THE CHARLATANS
NORTHWICH COUNTRY BOYS

PHOTOGRAPHIC CREDITS

FRONT COVER PHOTOGRAPH © DEREK RIDGERS, © LONDON FEATURES INTERNATIONAL LTD
© ALL ACTION
© LONDON FEATURES INTERNATIONAL LTD
© ANGELA LUBRANO
© REX FEATURES

Copyright © 1997 UFO MUSIC LTD

All rights reserved. Printed in Great Britain. No part of this book may be used or reproduced in any manner whatsoever without written permission except in the case of brief quotations embodied in critical articles or reviews.

UFO Music Ltd 18 Hanway Street London W1P 9DD England
Telephone: 0171 636 1281   Fax: 0171 636 0738

First published in Great Britain 1997
UFO Music Ltd 18 Hanway Street
London W1P 9DD

The author and publishers have made every effort to contact all copyright holders. Any who for any reason have not been contacted are invited to write to the publishers so that a full acknowledgment may be made in subsequent editions of this work.

ISBN 1-873884-91-5

Designed by UFO Music Ltd

THE CHARLATANS
NORTHWICH COUNTRY BOYS

Susan Wilson

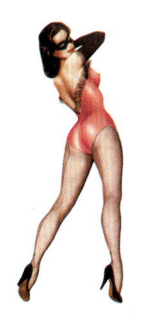

introduction

EVERYONE KNOWS HOW FICKLE THE ROCK INDUSTRY CAN BE. Fads spring up overnight, encouraged by shrewd business types, news-hungry journalists and musicians prepared to take a gamble on fame. Within a few months, the very same fads begin to fade, any excitement which whipped around them shrinks immeasurably and everyone's onto the next big thing. The casualties tend to be forgotten about at best, sneered at at worst while the survivors are awarded with heaps of respect and recognised as innovative scene-shifters. Occasionally though, a band gets caught in the middle.

When The Charlatans rose to fame back in 1990, they did so on a wave of Madchester fever. The Happy Mondays and the Stone Roses were transforming the face of rock culture, encouraging a whole generation of kids to grow floppy fringes and drop ecstasy tablets with their celebrated urban soundscapes. Indulgence was the finest form of escapism. Rock critic Jon Savage described the scene as *'a new pop bohemianism'* which hinged around a lifestyle that took in *'equal parts from the social organisation of the football terrace, from the holiday atmosphere of Ibizan clubs and from the mass transcendence of acid house parties,'* a lifestyle that balanced itself *'between ambition and solidarity, between radicalism and conservatism, between hedonism and idealism, between androgyny and laddishness, between gentleness and violence'*.

Writing for i-D magazine in 1990, Mike Noon outlined the sensibilities of the sprouting Scally scene in Manchester. The attitude was cynical and hard, the music a mixture of house and guitar bands, and all eyes were turning to the north for inspiration.

"We like the violence, we like getting off our heads, we like the dancing, the sweat," declared Wilbur of the Paris Angels, a Mancunion guitar band who resented being referred to as *'Scallies'*, preferring instead to be labelled Perry Boys, Boys or Firms. Acknowledging the significance of the Happy Mondays as representatives of their scene, the Angels were no doubt concerned that they were being misunderstood by a southern journalist sniffing for a story. They needn't have worried. London responded with bands like Flowered Up and a burgeoning club scene, but the Madchester label stuck and no one ever tried to dispute the origins of this europhic, if steel-edged development.

THE CHARLATANS
NORTHWICH COUNTRY BOYS

The Charlatans were based outside Manchester in Northwich, Cheshire, although three of their members were from the Midlands. Their links with this thriving scene were a little more tenuous than some, and this would actually count in their favour eventually, but back in the thick of it, they certainly benefited from their association with all things baggy.

"**People look back on that time and tend to remember the stupid clothes and stuff, but it was really important,**" singer Tim Burgess recalled to The Face In 1995. "**People gave up school or jobs and went out, took drugs and enjoyed themselves. It was a shock to the system.**"

"**I was only 21 when it was all happening and it was just great to be around making music,**" Tim later told Tammy Butt. "**It was really fun because everyone was just on for going out and enjoying themselves. Plus, it was new - Britpop isn't really a new phenomenon. Bands from that era like The Real People and James who are back in the spotlight, never really went away.**"

"**I think we added a lot of energy to that scene,**" drummer Jon Brookes told Sessions. "**I think we gave it an identity as much as other bands around at the same time. I think that we were instigators in that, and I feel really proud of that because it was a big thing that happened. And I think that *The Only One I Know* still stands up today as an all-time great. A bit of a garage classic on our behalf.**"

Exclusively working class in origin, Scally, baggy, Madchester, call it what you will, was a two-fingered gesture from the grit, the grime and the grins of the north to the fashion-conscious and moneyed south. Like all of its bands, The Charlatans had their feet on their ground and their heads on a roller-coaster. Unlike most of its bands, The Charlatans were destined for survival, and a history which although would be littered with problems and tragedy, would also sustain them in the face of anything life could throw at them. Their story is indeed a remarkable one.

Five

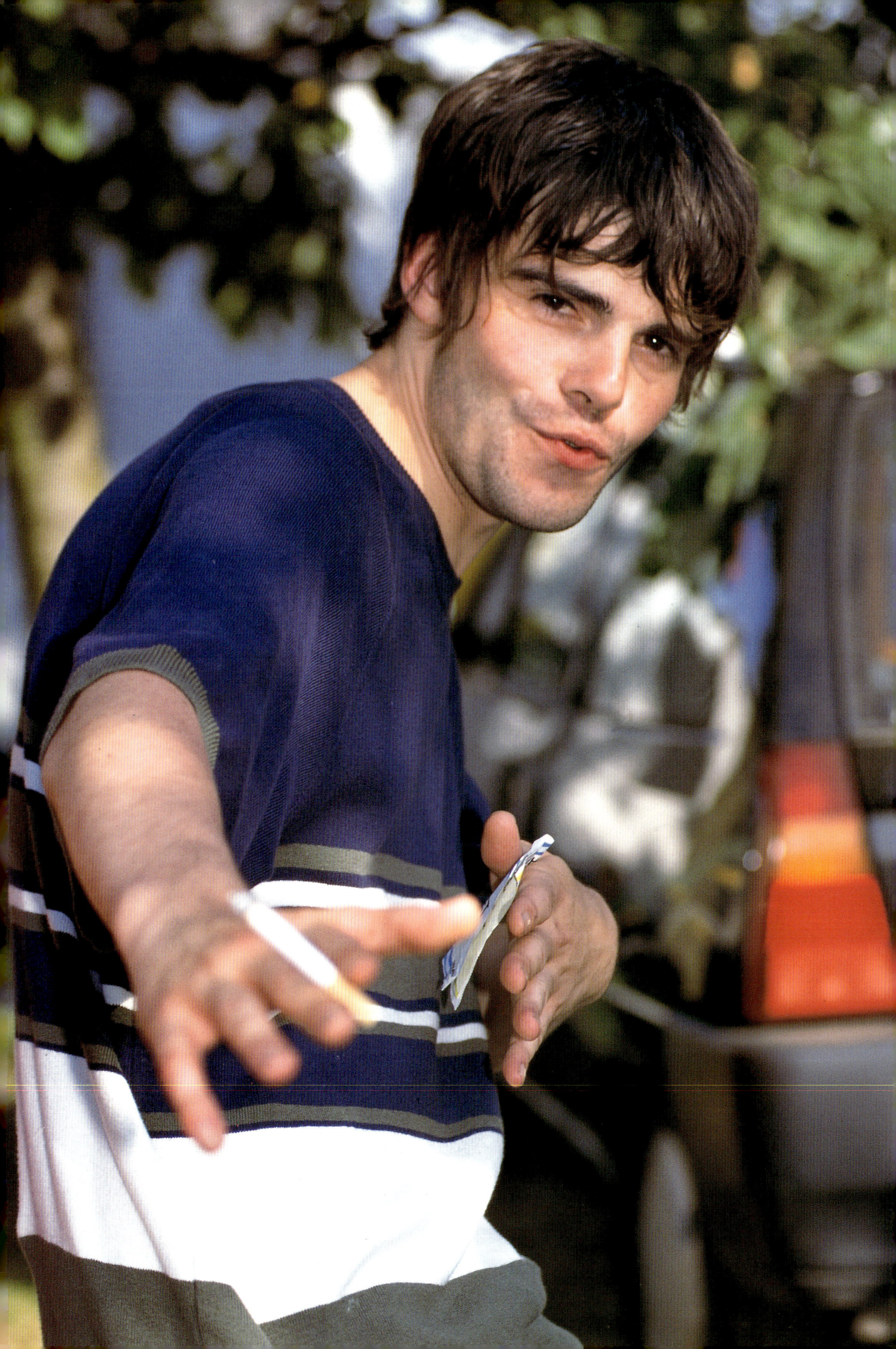

THE CHARLATANS
NORTHWICH COUNTRY BOYS

STORY NUMBER ONE

When he was just nine years old, Tim Burgess decided he wanted to be a pop star. Up until then, he'd assumed he'd end up working at ICI, the huge petrochemical plant which dominated the working lives of the majority of inhabitants of Northwich, his hometown in Cheshire. His dad worked there and all his neighbours worked there, so it seemed like the obvious option for his future. But when he was nine, Tim Burgess bought a record. It was his very first record and it was a song called 'Judith Says (Knock You In The Head)' by a band called The Vibrators. And when he was eleven he went to see Killing Joke wearing his school uniform. And after that, he wanted to be a pop star.

A year later another great impact was made on Tim by a record. Primal Scream's 'It Happens' was playing on John Peel's show, so he hiked off school to pick up a copy. And then he heard New Order and nothing was ever the same again. After that, Tim placed all his trust in his favourite bands. He'd come home from school, go up to his bedroom and listen to music all night. He'd make up imaginary set lists for imaginary New Order and Fall gigs, working out his ideal selections. He tried to take guitar lessons from his bass-playing uncle once he'd made up his mind to try his hand at the pop business, but his impatience, and a supernatural experience got the better of him so he quit.

"**I was messing around on this Ouija board,**" he told the NME's Paul Moody in 1995. "**We'd got this war veteran giving us messages and everything he said was spot on. I asked him what groups I liked and he spelt out JOY 4TIM which I took to be Joy Division, who I loved. But then I asked if I'd ever be a famous guitarist and he said no and it really threw me. What really scared me was that I was going out with this girl at the time and this spirit said he was coming back the next year as her baby. That really frightened me. We split up just after that, but a year later she had a kid and if things had gone differently that could have been me.**"

Seven

STORY NUMBER ONE

"**I was obsessed with guitarists,**" Tim told i-D's Dave Simpson. "**But I tried to learn and I just couldn't do it. I never had a lead singer as a hero, really. Bernard Sumner was probably the first person I thought was amazing, and maybe Ian Curtis.**"

Deterred from the life of a guitar god, Tim carried on buying records. And he started hanging round one local record shop in particular, like all kids who are into music do. Called Omega Records, the shop was run by Steve Harrison with whom Tim quickly became friendly and the pair started going to see bands together.

Meanwhile, at school, Tim had been continuing to struggle. He just didn't like it. He was good at sports, and was captain of both the football and rugby teams, but academically he couldn't give a stuff. He managed to wangle his way into woodwork and metalwork classes in the mornings, and then played sport in the afternoons, but that was it really. Not that academic success seemed terribly important when you received the sort of career advice Tim did anyway. One day, his whole class were dealt out sheets of paper face down like in an exam. The teacher announced "**A few of you girls may get jobs in shops. The rest of you had better fill out these.**" Tim turned his sheet over to discover an unemployment benefit claim form. He left school that year with one 'O'level in English and a pocket full of dreams.

Having been told by his teachers that he stood no chance of doing anything with his life, Tim at least ended up out of the dole queue. At school he'd been hanging out with hard kids, making them laugh to avoid getting beaten up. He'd been nicked for stealing, but he still managed to get a foot on the ladder, even if it was at ICI. His dreams, for the time being at least, were to stay firmly locked into his pocket as the dreaded petrochemical plant beckoned, and before he knew it he was licking stamps in the mail room and cycling round between factories delivering parcels and letters. But Tim, ever the optimist, later confessed to liking this mind-numbingly monotonous task. He even ended up becoming what he later described as "**a bit of a jobsworth**".

Eight

THE CHARLATANS
NORTHWICH COUNTRY BOYS

"I liked it 'cos it made me really bored," he told The Face in September 1996. "While I was sticking envelopes down I used to daydream about all the records I'd buy at the weekend. I had this image of Jimmy from 'Quadrophenia' in my head and dreamed of the day when I could tell them all to shove it like he did."

"I did work for five years in the end after leaving school," he told the NME's Paul Moody. "First of all I did the mail, just like in 'Quadrophenia'. I had this bicycle with a sack on the front and I'd ride around the factory doling out letters to everybody; it was a real laugh. But after two years of that you had to change and I had to clean the toilets and all the lockers and stuff. It was either that or become a bricklayer's mate or do the drains."

"The thing is I wasn't pissed off doing it because I got on with people and I liked the money. Every Thursday, when I got my wages, I wouldn't even go out drinking. I'd just buy records, some 'Nuggets' compilation or dance stuff, and sit in me room playing them all the following week."

In time Tim found himself scrubbing out the insides of chemical tanks and asbestos-coated ceilings.

"I had to sign a contract," he told Melody Maker's Stud Brothers in 1995, "so that if I die of asbestos me mum and dad or me sister can have a four-year legal battle for a load of dosh."

Two years after Tim quit his job, a certain Liam Gallagher ended up in exactly the same hazardous position.

Despite the unpleasant but necessary business of earning a living, Tim carried on dreaming,

Nine

STORY NUMBER ONE

cut his hair, bought a leather jacket and began to act out his Iggy Pop fantasies with a local band called The Electric Crayons.

Playing things like 'Cold Metal' by Iggy, and Led Zeppelin numbers with his band, Tim actually became Mr Pop in his mind. Those moments on stage where he yelled and screamed and strutted, he knew this was what he could do, and he knew he was cool. After all, he wasn't born with those lips and those hips for nothing.

Around about the same time, Steve Harrison was being hassled by five guys, Baz Kettley, Martin Blunt, Jon Baker, Rob Collins and Jon Brookes. From the ashes of Martin's band, the Gift Horses (for whom Jon Brookes also played), Rob and Martin had formed a band called The Charlatans and they wanted Steve to manage them. Tim and Steve decided to go along to one of their gigs and see what they were up to, and Tim's first thoughts were that they could do with a more dynamic singer.

An interesting lot they were, these Charlatans. Bassist Martin was a mod boy with a passion for Motown and a very quiet nature, major Who fan Rob had begrudgingly learnt to play the Hammond organ as a kid with his dad but was glad he'd persevered now, and drummer Jon Brookes was into reggae and hard rock. They'd been together as a band for about a year, and when they lost their singer, Baz, Martin, who knew Steve through the mod scene, asked him if he knew of any possible replacements. Steve immediately thought of his mate Tim, the cool frontman who was currently Iggying it up locally so he set up an audition in Walsall.

Initially things didn't go too well. Tim was so embroiled in his Iggy act that he actually couldn't sing properly. He was shouting and striking all the poses for all he was worth, but he wasn't giving The Charlatans any idea as to whether he could do this for real. So they stopped, Martin had a go, insisted that this obviously charismatic guy calm down and focus on the task in hand, and they started again. Second time around, Tim felt his way into the beats far more comfortably. Within a matter of moments it became apparent that without all the acting up, here was a frontman for The Charlatans.

THE CHARLATANS
NORTHWICH COUNTRY BOYS

Finally Tim had found a band who were as disillusioned as he was with crap jobs and mundane existences. They were all equally serious about breaking into the big time, and so over their first summer together, they committed themselves to writing songs. They jammed endlessly, conjuring up tunes - once as many as four in one weekend - and they weren't just half hearted tunes either. They were pretty darn good. One in particular, 'The Only One I Know' stood out, begging to be let loose into the world, and by now Tim was convinced that his band were going to be bigger than New Order.

Soon The Charlatans were ready to play before any public who'd listen. Gigs were arranged in their locality, Tim kept a diary of them and Steve began to plug the band to all of his Omega customers. By now he'd begun managing them as well.

When 'The Only One I Know' got its first live airing, it was nothing short of a resounding success and convinced everyone in the band that they were really onto something. A gig supporting Cactus World News at the Manchester Boardwalk further served to boost their confidence. Out of the 210 strong audience, only 10 bothered to stay to listen to the headlining act.

By now, the baggy scene was in full swing in Manchester. Bands like the Paris Angels, Northside, the Inspiral Carpets, and of course the Stone Roses and the Happy Mondays were spreading the word but while The Charlatans had definite links with the scene, specialising, as they did, in groove-orientated dance rock, they couldn't find themselves a record deal. In the end they decided to release 'Indian Rope' on their own label, Dead Dead Good Records. It made number one in the indie charts and sold out of the first pressing within just one week.

In 1995 Jon Brookes told Select's Clark Collis how he felt when he saw the news on his band on The Chart Show for the first time.

Eleven

STORY NUMBER ONE

"I was at home and I'd put on The Chart Show. I knew it was out and I knew it had done well. But when they said it was number one I went fucking mad. I did a lap of honour in the front room. We didn't have a video, but it was more romantic because they had a still of the first sleeve which was a picture of me playing the drums. It looked like some mad garage kid smashing the shit out of his drums. I had to put the kettle on immediately."

Such unexpected success naturally attracted the attention of the music press. Soon journalists were nitpicking Tim who responded by baffling them all with muso ramblings about Sly and the Family Stone and The Rolling Stones, and God knows how many bands from the past who no one was familiar with. He also declared that The Charlatans were the best band, and that everyone else was rubbish. The press started to flow.

Soon, the band jacked in their jobs, and turned to full-time musicianship. In his interview with Select, Jon Brookes explained how he quit mediocre employment.

"I was working as a wood machinist, processing wood for kitchen units. (In his spare time he made drumsticks). Every week I'd have a couple of days off to play a gig in Crewe or somewhere. I said to the boss, 'Look man I've got to have two days off this week.' He said, 'You know what you're doing and if you take two days off then don't come back'. I just got me coat, man, and said 'I'll see you on TV'. And it fucking worked! I felt like Clint Eastwood."

When he was 18, Jon had spent a brief spell in London, staying in a caravan at Crystal Palace drumming with some mates. They had a publishing deal, but he never really understood their music.

"I knew it was crap but I didn't know why," he informed the Stud Brothers. He disappeared back to Manchester, stopping off at Ibiza on the way, dyed his hair yellow and resumed playing with Martin.

Twelve

THE CHARLATANS
NORTHWICH COUNTRY BOYS

Thirteen

STORY NUMBER ONE

Whereas before, The Charlatans couldn't get a label to so much as sniff at their heels, now A&R people were clamouring for them. The usual tempting offers poured in - all manner of gifts, free breakfasts, lunches and dinners, so the band decided to decline all of them, and opted for a label interested in them for the right reasons. Beggars Banquet won out, and a deal was signed at Jon's house in Wednesbury over a pile of cheese sandwiches.

The first single Beggars put out was 'The Only One I Know'. It rushed into the indie charts at number one, and landed up in the top five in the nationals, closely followed by 'Then'. An offer to appear on Top Of The Pops was turned down because the band were "on tour in the Outer Hebrides or something" but their successes continued and their debut album, 'Some Friendly' entered the charts at number one.

After their UK success, a tour of America was planned and undertaken, leading to a lawsuit with the original American sixties Charlatans, forcing the Brits to stick a qualifying UK on the end of their name, and Tim, of course, went AWOL in the desert. The band toured Japan, Jon bought himself a Mercedes and finally, everyone fled for much deserved holidays.

"We're not even successful yet," said Tim at the time. **"We've got a lot more to achieve before we auto-destruct."**

In 1991, things looked to be going extraordinarily well for The Charlatans. But unbeknown to anyone, a heap of trouble was just around the corner. Baggy was going bad. The Happy Mondays imploded, and the Stone Roses seemed to be spending most of their time in court or the recording studio. The lively, happy vibe was fizzling out, and with all eyes turned to The Charlatans to keep the torch burning, the pressure was on.

Around this time though, Martin began to fall into a depression. He became very withdrawn and eventually ended up having to be hospitalised. He'd do weird things, like go out for a tin of dog food and come back with a month's supply of cat food.

Fourteen

THE CHARLATANS
NORTHWICH COUNTRY BOYS

"**I lost three months,**" he told i-D's Dave Simpson. "**I remember going out for a drink with him, and in four hours he hadn't said a word to me or drunk an inch from his beer.**"

Martin's breakdown weakened the band's position, but it wasn't the only misfortune to befall them.

When The Charlatans started to demo their new material, Beggars Banquet pointed out that it might be a good idea if they could come up with another 'The Only One I Know'. They wanted a good commercial groove to brighten up the charts and boost the band's career again, but as Tim pointed out, making music really doesn't happen that way. At least not unless you're in some formulaic pop band willing to churn out hit singles like pies on a factory conveyor belt. The Charlatans were a band with soul, they couldn't write to order, but while they tried to explain this to their label, they were met with deaf ears.

More was still to come. Towards the end of the year, the band played the Royal Albert Hall. The gig was stupendous with thousands of kids rocking the joint, E'ed out of their minds, but the bombshell fell the next day when guitarist Jon Baker announced that he was leaving. Later, to Select, Martin drily commented "**He's probably in a potting shed now. He was always a big gardener. Always tending his greens.**" Baker's reasons were in reality the usual - he simply couldn't handle the lack of privacy, and the pressures of playing with the band were getting to him.

Rumours started flying about the band splitting up. But before long they'd recruited a new boy, Mark Collins. A Mancunion, Mark had spent some of his schooldays sat next to Bonehead who was later to play with Oasis. He'd also been as troubled in his teens as Tim.

"**I was the shortest person at school,**" he told i-D. "**Four foot six until I was 16. No one ever bullied me 'cos they thought I was strange. I was hardly in class, I refused to go. I had me own social worker at 14 and was taken out of school.**"

Fifteen

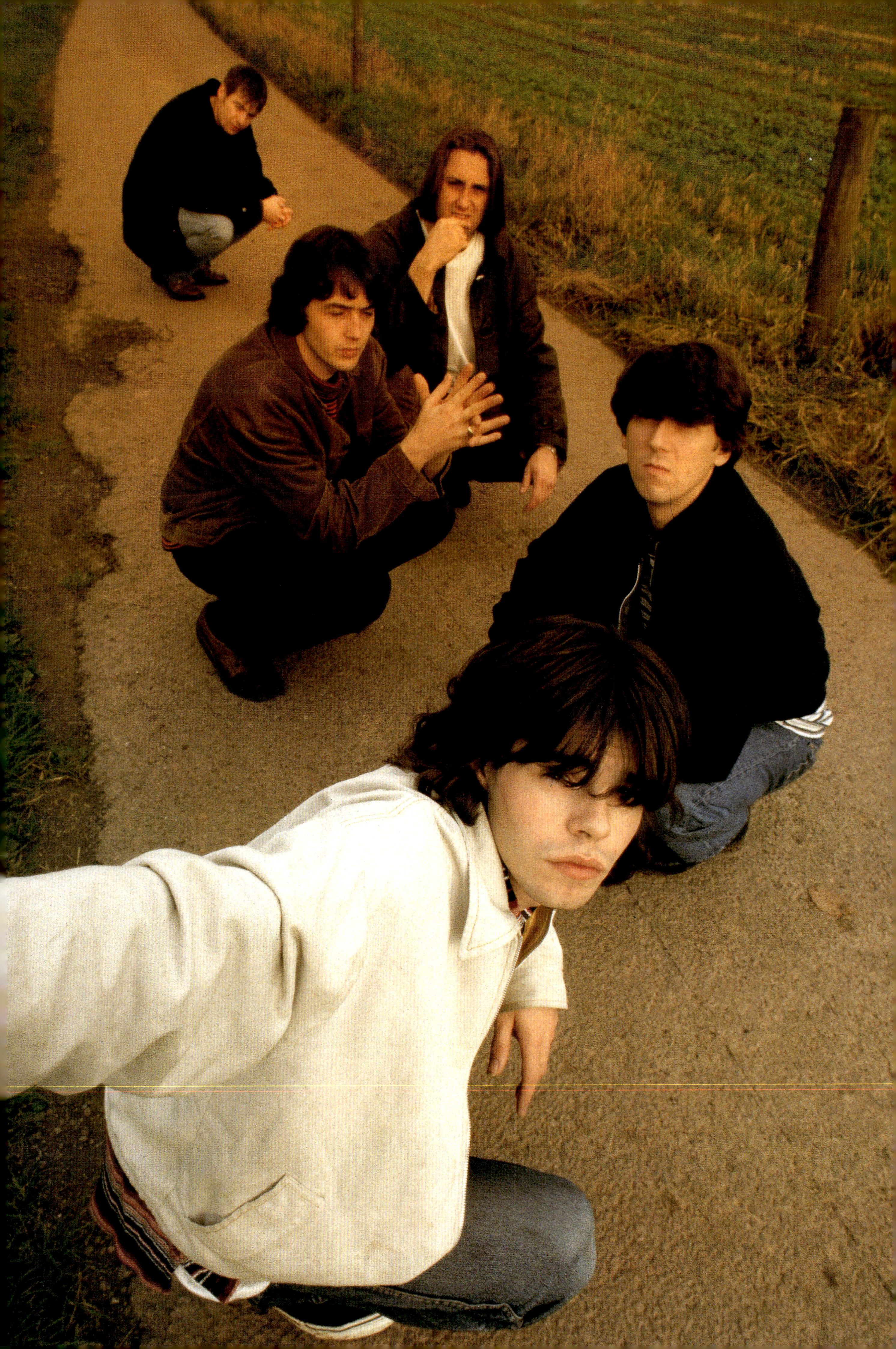

THE CHARLATANS
NORTHWICH COUNTRY BOYS

"There was a lot of Catholic shit going on. It was a school run by Brothers and I used to get called into the headmaster's for a 'hug'. I didn't like that. That was another reason I didn't attend school. I mean, he didn't touch me, exactly. He'd just hug me, and I was dead little so he was hugging me sort of around there, going 'so Mark, you're having a few problems at school?' and I was thinking, 'you're my biggest problem at school'."

Eventually Mark was sent for an IQ test and achieved a high result. He was re-installed at school with instructions for the teachers to leave him well alone. His final year was spent drawing on his desk and then, he discovered music. He was to have a very instrumental role in The Charlatans.

"Right from when I first joined the band I've been a lippy bastard," Mark told Melody Maker's Paul Mathur in 1995. "I didn't want to just go in and stand quietly at the back letting everyone else decide what we were going to do. I wanted to be able to play a part in all this."

"I used to be in a band called The Waltones, and we played a lot but it was obvious it was never going to be huge. Then I got a phone call from the manager of Inspiral Carpets and he said there was a vacancy in The Charlatans. I'd got a couple of their singles so I went for the job. Noel was working for the Inspirals at the time so I guess the manager could have asked him instead and he might have been doing what I'm doing now."

"I always had the idea that The Charlatans were all from Northwich. No one told me most of them were from The Black Country. I spent the first six months getting Tim to translate everything they said."

Mark knew the Inspiral Carpets because he'd driven their van for them and worked on their backline. Prior to that he'd spent eight years on the dole, and a bizarre spell in a kebab house

Seventeen

STORY NUMBER ONE

where he'd create kebabs out of frozen mince by crushing it into little balls with his bare hands. A man who claims to have been born with four kidneys, his character, not to mention his guitar playing, added a valuable new dimension to The Charlatans.

So finally it was into the studio to make the difficult second album. At the production helm was Flood, famous for his work with U2 (and hosts of others these days), but while his ideas were interesting and he obviously knew what he was doing, somehow things never quite gelled.

"Flood was really good," recalled Rob to Clark Collis, **"But in the end it didn't really sound like us. I remember him trying some stuff out and it just sounded like Dr Who's Tardis. He got pissed off with me one day because he'd spent three days mixing this song and getting all the faders in the right place on the mixing desk. I came in and pulled the switches down. He got so angry. I was pissed up. I didn't know."**

Mark remembered it, again to Collis, as a **"fucking nightmare. Martin was going through a rough time. He was a bit depressed and wasn't talking. So I'm thinking, is this my fault? I thought I'd jinxed them. I became an alcoholic within about six months. One night we were doing a session for the album down at Rockfield and I drank so much I completely missed 24 hours and woke up pissing blood."**

The album sessions were resumed once Martin had recovered enough to start communicating again, and Mark quit drowning his liver. No one felt terribly sure of Flood's production, confirming Rob's doubts, but they did feel confident of their songs, and in March 1992, 'Between 10th And 11th' was released.

By this time, rock culture had taken another swerve. The hedonistic dancing days of Madchester had given way to an influx of flannel shirted, guitar toting grunge bands from America's northwest coast. Nirvana, Soundgarden, Pearl Jam, Mudhoney, Alice In Chains, Screaming

Eighteen

THE CHARLATANS
NORTHWICH COUNTRY BOYS

Nineteen

STORY NUMBER ONE

Trees and Tad were making the news and baggy was consigned to a hazy, glistening memory. The Summer of Love had collapsed beneath the weight of its own indulgences and a new, more politically correct, even po faced genre, fuelled by the same raw energy as punk was in its place. For a band like The Charlatans this wasn't altogether good news, because although Tim had denied any close links with baggy and Madchester, they were definitely associated with the scene. Needless to say, their second album wasn't warmly received.

"We really wanted to make a record that was a bit different," Tim told Sun Zoom Spark in 1995. **"We knew people expected great things from us and our way of dealing with that was to go in a different direction and be a bit experimental. I think we almost couldn't handle it. We were so scared of blowing it that we panicked."**

'Between 10th And 11th' entered the national charts at number 21. Rob Collins was completely non-plussed, having already predicted a backlash. The others maintain that they didn't care either, but in conversation with Select's Clark Collis, Rob confessed that he was gutted.

"Some of the reviews were just ridiculous. One said, 'There's no tune, no song, no chorus, no melody. And no verse. That was the whole review. I thought, Fuck it. This is one man's opinion. It's just a shame that one hundred thousand people are going to read it."

Later, in an interview with Melody Maker's Paul Mathur, Tim confessed that he didn't really like his girlfriend of the time listening to the album. Then again, he didn't really like anyone listening to it.

"I can see how much better we we could have done it, but at the time we felt we were doing the best we could."

Whatever the critics had to say, and however they may have felt about 'Between 10th And 11th' in the future, at the time The Charlatans still had tour obligations to fulfil, and that

Twenty

THE CHARLATANS
NORTHWICH COUNTRY BOYS

summer when they played New York, Tim grabbed the opportunity to call Madonna *"an ugly fucker"* when she showed up.

"We'd just done this gig at the Limelight," Tim told Collis, **"And Madonna walks in with Seymour Stein. I'm just lying on the dressing room floor. She looks at me and says I'm gross. And I said, 'Yeah, well you're an ugly fucker and your videos are stupid'. No, actually I said that I thought the first three tracks on her album were smart. But then I say that to everyone."**

Swallowing their pride, The Charlatans put the whole unsavoury experience of the second album to the backs of their minds. They weren't going to be deterred so easily. They had more than that to prove, so they simply decided to plough straight on with the third album. This time, it was Martin who really began pulling things together. Having been so heavily withdrawn, and eventually ill with the second album, he was determined to get a creative hold on its successor, and with Tim he set about writing songs. Flood was lined up to produce, but he couldn't fit the band in, which, considering everyone's feelings on the production of 'Between 10th And 11th' was probably a good thing. Instead, Steve Hillage of the classic weirdo hippy band Gong, and System 7 was roped in.

Hillage had been deluging Steve Harrison with requests to produce the band. He wanted to capture them live, and believed that until they managed to accurately reproduce their live sound and atmosphere on record, they wouldn't get there. The band agreed.

With a solid future plan beginning to take shape, things were looking up for The Charlatans. But their troubled times were far from over, and the biggest blip to date was just about to stain everything.

On December 3rd 1992, Rob Collins, always a bit of a loose cannon to say the least, found himself at the wheel of a getaway car at an armed robbery. Later, he would admit that his actions were "really stupid", but considering they landed him in jail, that was something of an understatement.

Twenty One

**STORY
NUMBER ONE**

**THE CHARLATANS
NORTHWICH COUNTRY BOYS**

The Charlatans had just completed a tour of Japan and Rob and a friend of his were on their way to visit Jon. On the way, Rob's mate stopped off and held up an off-licence. Rob should have buggered off, but he didn't because you don't do that to mates, so instead he was nicked, sent to court in September 1993 and found himself lumbered with an eight month prison sentence. In the event he only served four months, sharing a cell at Shrewsbury prison with a man who had murdered his wife and stabbed her father. His introduction to life inside consisted of watching someone having boiling water thrown in their face. When a bloke approached him in the showers he thought it was all over, but instead of what he was dreading, the inmate simply whistled 'The Only One I Know' and said **"Good band mate."** Fortunately, Rob's pop star status served to alleviate him from the usual traumas inflicted by prisoners upon each other, so while his four months wasn't exactly a holiday, it was a lot better than it could have been.

Nevertheless, Rob's incarceration was an almighty setback for the band. Prior to his sentence, The Charlatans, although not quite able to face up to the fact that their keyboard player might actually be imprisoned, laid down as many keyboard tracks and backing vocals as they could.

"We turned the corner when Rob went into prison," Tim told i-D in 1995. **"We were terrified, the worst of it was waiting. He got arrested in December '92 but didn't go inside until October '93. So we had all that time. We'd started writing for 'Up To Our Hips' and it was going slow. Rob gets arrested and we're writing and it was weird 'cos we didn't know how long he was gonna get. We heard that he might get five years, and that would have been the end of the group."**

"We hated him for jeopardising the group. When he came out he was really withdrawn and found it hard to get back into the band. We were pretty hard on him, actually."

Twenty Three

STORY NUMBER ONE

"There was no questioning our loyalty," Martin told the NME in 1995. "It's just standing by your mates. Prison really stripped Rob of his pride. He lost a lot. His wife abandoned him and he doesn't get to see his kid now. A lot of his friends didn't stand by him either. We were the ones who were writing to him and sending tapes."

"He didn't even know if he was still going to be in the band when he came out. He got what he deserved, probably could have got a longer stretch, but he did his time for the band because he believes in us and we believe in him. Anyway we played 'Top Of The Pops' the day after he was released and that was him back in the fold in style."

"He never told us whether he did it or not," Tim admitted in yet another interview in 1995. "He did say that any dignity or self-respect you have is stripped from you while you're in there. When he came out he had a general apathy with the world. He gave less of a fuck about anything."

Speaking to Clark Collis, Rob recalled how he felt after his release.

"I came out on January 15th and we were on 'Top Of The Pops' on the 24th. I could just imagine them all inside watching the TV going 'You fucking wanker'. I have managed to put most of it behind me, but every now and again it keeps coming back. When we were playing at Glastonbury someone started shouting 'Jailbait! Jailbait!'. I went 'What the fuck are you on about? SHUT UP!"

While Rob was in jail, Tim couldn't face visiting him. He probably couldn't cope with what had really happened, and simply felt, understandably, let down, as indeed did all of the band. Nevertheless, they carried on. For the new album, Martin stepped in, where previously Rob had been at the controls. The Stud Brothers described Martin as being the man most

Twenty Four

THE CHARLATANS
NORTHWICH COUNTRY BOYS

concerned with the continuation of The Charlatans, and consequently, the resultant album was a bass-heavy, dance-trip affair, built around a deeper groove than the band had previously exhibited. In short it was quite brilliant, being a back to the roots, full-on rock-funk extravaganza, which produced some stunning singles, including 'Can't Get Out Of Bed' and 'Jesus Hairdo'. It reached number eight in the national charts, a notable improvement sales-wise than its predecessor.

Steve Hillage had proved to be a wise choice of producer. Jon recalled to Clark Collis that he'd really buzzed off the band's music, and that they were all getting into different types of tunes, like The Faces and Funkadelic.

"One day someone brought in 'The Flying Teapot' (a somewhat absurd Gong record from the 1970s) and we couldn't stop laughing. There was this feeling of all or nothing. But it was also like, 'Right, let's fucking show them'."

Which is exactly what they did. Naturally though, criticisms were made.

"Some bastard journalist slagged off 'Up To Our Hips' by saying that we sound like we're just making records for the money," Tim complained to Sun Zoom Spark in 1995. **"I thought you prick! Come to fucking Trentham Gardens (where the band played a triumphant gig in 1994) and then say that. No one could see us play a gig and say we're crap. I defy anyone to do that."**

Speaking about the actual album, Tim was obviously indignant about the ways in which some people might interpret the song titles. At the time one of the media buzzwords was 'Generation X', a term employed by journalists and youth culture commentators to describe the slacker nation which had developed out of an apathy brought about the bleak existence afforded by a Tory government to its up and coming youth. Slackers grew up not caring about anything or anyone, but Tim, a man who might easily be described as one of life's biggest enthusiasts, wasn't having any of it.

Twenty Five

STORY
NUMBER ONE

"This Generation X thing is shite. I'm not a part of it 'cos I've got enthusiasm for life. People think that because we call songs things like 'Can't Get Out Of Bed' and 'Easy Life' that we're a lazy bunch of miserable bastards, but 'Easy Life' is about not wanting an easy life. There's got to be excitement. I did like Nirvana but I never felt part of that whole slacker thing. I've always been hyperactive."

Later, in an interview with the NME, Tim divulged that 'Easy Life' was in fact about Rob.

"That line, 'shoot it up, let's go for a ride' was about the robbery, and I think I was trying to capture part of what he's all about with that song. Basically he's just into kicks, no matter what it takes. My picture of Rob is that it doesn't matter that he plays the keyboard - even though he's brilliant at it - for him the thrill is just being on a stage where things might go wrong. He just likes danger. He's the only person I've ever known who's into bungee jumping and stuff like that..."

While 'Up To Our Hips' didn't exactly rock the nation, it did go some way towards re-establishing The Charlatans as an act to be reckoned with. They were still delivering the goods, still hitting the charts with their singles, and they'd managed to score a top ten album. But they really didn't make the most of it, essentially throwing away what was, in fact, a brilliant record. Two singles, a handful of gigs, and then a short tour of the States was just about all the promotion afforded by the band to their third album.

"In America," Tim told the Stud Brothers in 1995, "we found that the gigs had only been advertised about a week before we got there, so they hadn't sold out. We'd been selling out everywhere, big time, for four years, so really it was the first time it felt like a struggle. And also, even though we were pleased with 'Up To Our Hips', some of it was brilliant, we just felt we had a better album in us right then. So we thought, fuck it, let's just go back and make another album."

Back to the studio then.

Twenty Six

THE CHARLATANS
NORTHWICH COUNTRY BOYS

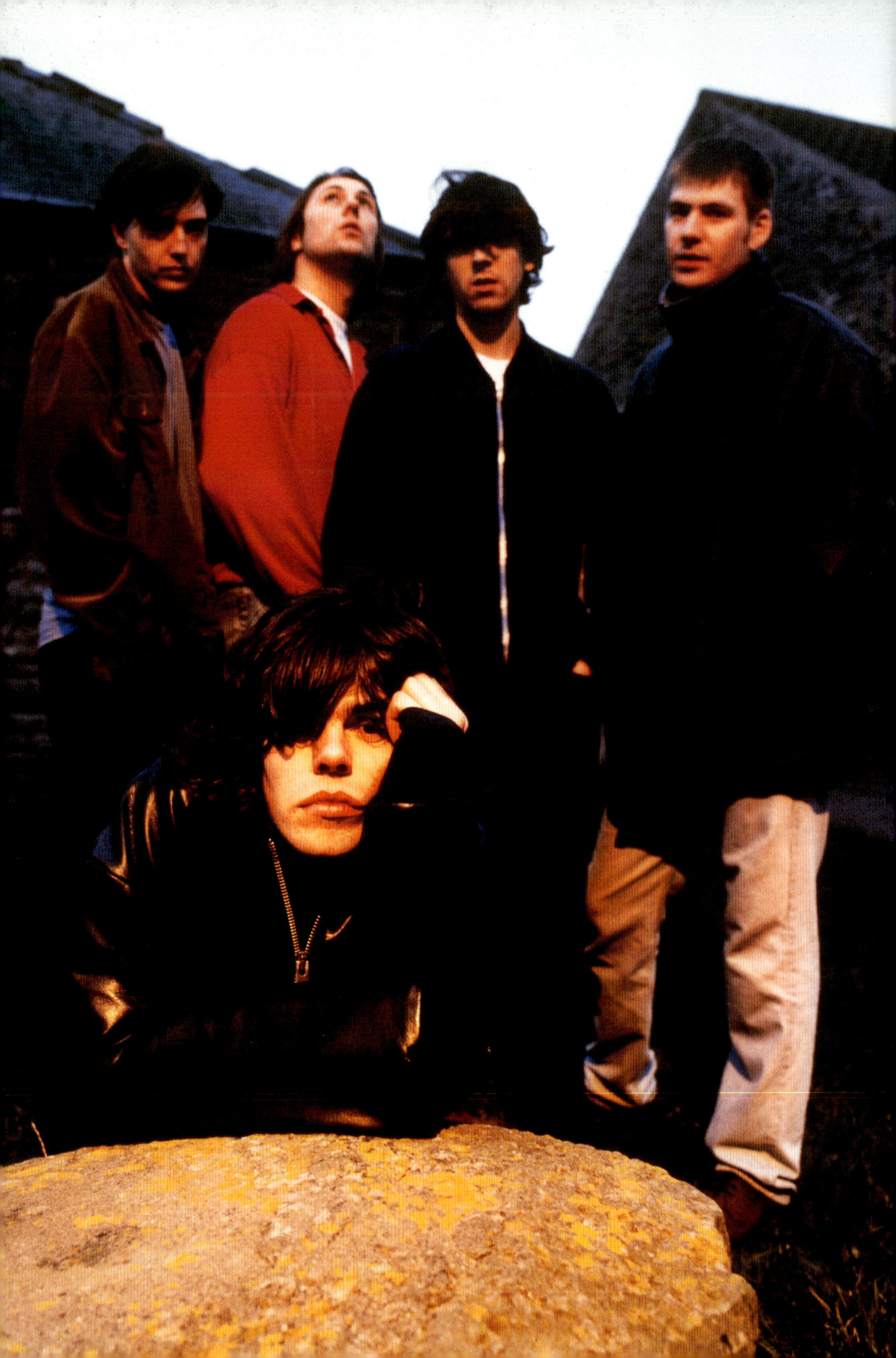

THE CHARLATANS
NORTHWICH COUNTRY BOYS

STORY NUMBER TWO

With the relative success of 'Up To Our Hips' behind them, The Charlatans were in fine fettle when it came to preparation for their next album. They approached it in a relaxed manner, and any problems which cropped up along the way were dealt with and put behind them. **"The album was conceived on a lilo in the Mediterranean,"** Mark Collins told i-D, once *'The Charlatans'* was released. **"We had a week off and took our girlfriends. We decided we didn't want any downers on the album. Everything was looking right for the group."**

Despite what Mark said, the new album actually evolved in a more structured manner than anything the band had previously done. Mark spent time in London with Tim Burgess, writing songs with a guitar, a drum machine and a 4-track, and sleeping on his floor.

"We'd set ourselves challenges," the guitarist told Danny Eccleston. **"We'd say, 'Right, we're going to write eight songs in a week' and I didn't leave until we had eight songs - even if only two were any good! We managed to get about 30 tunes together. They're still all credited to all five of us, though, 'cos that's how it works. Even if we've taken full melodies and chord structures to the group, the flesh they put on them is as important."**

Tim's vast record collection also provided inspiration.

"Being at Tim's is like being at a record library," Mark informed Eccleston. **"He's got thousands and thousands of records - any piece of music you could ever want to listen to. This album was inspired by loads of stuff from The Beatles to The Stones, Beck to The Who, Small Faces, Beastie Boys, Led Zeppelin to The Beach Boys - especially the 'Holland' and 'Surf's Up' era."**

Tim had also got heavily into hip hop, especially the Wu Tang Clan, and would play the records over and over again to anyone who spent time round at his North London flat.

Twenty Nine

**STORY
NUMBER TWO**

Thirty

THE CHARLATANS
NORTHWICH COUNTRY BOYS

Once the songs were finished, The Charlatans spent six months writing and recording their self titled album in a residential studio in Monnow Valley, Monmouth, Wales. They captured their good moods on vinyl by playing football, and going out and caning it, and coming back to the studio with whatever juices or substances they'd consumed, still careering round their systems. Half a decade on from their initial associations with the Madchester E scene, the band were still operating under the influence.

"Is it a celebration?" asked Mark of the new album in the i-D interview, **"Well, there were a lot of parties going down. We spent an extra month in the studio 'cos we were having such a good time. We did a lot of drugs on this LP. When you're locked away for three months, it's like...you can lose your mind on tour in America, but you can lose your mind in the studio as well. I like that, as long as it comes out on the record. Jon (Brookes) was obsessed, going through a voodoo phase. We had a huge bong surrounded by religious symbols and everything. We prayed to the bong."**

In an interview with the NME's Johnny Cigarettes, Tim embellished this story.

"There was this guy who hangs round the studio who's got pleurisy and a collapsed lung from doing too much bong. He ended up in hospital again and one of our mates took him a portable bong in there! Ha ha! Fucking mad for it he was!"

Tim also recalled how heavily into ecstasy he'd been in 1991, 1992.

"I probably took it every day for a couple of months. We knew this chemist who could get us pure MDMA when we were in America - you've got to have a bit of that! But... I don't do much of that anymore. I did speed and coke for a while, but somehow that just neutralises my energy and makes me like everyone else when they're sober!"

Thirty One

**STORY
NUMBER TWO**

"You should see that bastard on E," chipped in Mark, "He's impossible to shut up. He'll be there at the stereo, putting a thousand records on a minute. Like an extreme version of what he is now. But we aren't that big on drugs anymore as a band. I was a bit of a coke fiend in America, mind - I can only smoke it now, because my nose is so fucked!"

"Without wanting to harp on about drugs, I think you can tell the difference between American and British groups," Mark told i-D in a slightly different vein. "Ecstasy never happened in a big way in America. They're all into smack out there and you can tell, man, it shows in the music, and it's all 'I'm so miserable I wanna put a bullet to my head', and we're so happy we wanna dance all night, man! Fuck being miserable. Life's too short."

Although he went on to add, "There's nothing on any of our records which says 'go out and take drugs'. We've got a reputation as a party band but I always thought we were miserable bastards until we turned the corner."

The corner Mark was referring to was Rob Collins' arrest. It was the biggest hurdle the band had ever had to clear, and once they had, they were determined not to let anything get in their way. Not even a couple of injuries and a producer problem....

Steve Hillage had been drafted in to help the band record their album, but halfway through the sessions, everyone realised things weren't going brilliantly, so they parted company with him. Later, in a Melody Maker news story, Tim claimed that he thought 'Up To Our Hips' was rubbish (although he meant compared to what was about to come) and Hillage understandably wasn't too pleased. But during the recording of the album, Hillage had also been contracted to other jobs, leaving the band slightly pissed off with someone who wasn't completely committed to them. He also wanted to rush them. So they sacked him.

Thirty Two

THE CHARLATANS
NORTHWICH COUNTRY BOYS

"The record label actually suggested that we were more than capable of producing ourselves," an incredulous Mark explained to Eccleston. **"I'm not sure if that's them being stingy bastards or whether they have total faith in us."**

Rather than take the risk of leaving themselves to their own devices, The Charlatans held onto their engineer, Dave Charles, and came up with what was later to be described as a "killer" album.

"Dave Charles is one of the best engineers in Britain," Mark explained to Danny Eccleston. **"He's old school. He knows what a live feel is all about. Hillage had a bit of a techno head on him which wasn't a bad thing, 'cos now we've got a bit of both. It was the best time I've ever had making a record though - no one was in hospital or jail! I love Monnow Valley to death. All I need to do is raise half a million quid and I could buy the place!"**

As for the couple of injuries, Jon Brookes managed to break his ankle playing football, just before the band were due to record the last two tracks, and Rob broke his hand dragging his keyboard roadie through a door in a nightclub. **"That's the sort of luck we have,"** noted Mark at the time.

Still, everyone ploughed on, and the end result more than paid off. When they emerged from the Welsh valleys, The Charlatans came back bearing an album worth more than its weight in gold. It was the album which would completely revive their career, putting them back on the map as one of Britain's best bands of the decade.

"They've certainly matured," said the band's manager, Steve Harrison in an interview with Music Week's Stephen Worthy when 'The Charlatans' was released. **"'Some Friendly' reflected what was going on in Manchester at the time - a very exciting time. I think 'Between 10th And 11th' became very exploratory as Flood, the producer, came from a technology-based background."**

Thirty Three

STORY NUMBER TWO

"'Up To Our Hips' started realising the potential of the band, but at this time the UK media hadn't caught up with us. What's helped sustain it is probably one of the most loyal and partisan fanbases that any band has in the UK."

Three singles were released from the album; 'Just Lookin', 'Crashin' In' and 'Just When You're Thinkin' Things Over'. And when the album was launched onto Great Britain, the rock record buying public responded by tipping it into the number one slot. When they found out about their latest triumph, the band were in Nottingham, and so they headed for the nearest pub to neck beer, vodka, champagne and Hooch. They could barely believe it but it was finally official - THE CHARLATANS WERE BACK.

"It's mad," said a stunned and delirious Tim to Melody Maker's Paul Mathur at the time. "I just keep going round saying to everyone, 'We're Number One'. If I say it enough, then eventually I'm going to believe it myself. It feels fucking brilliant. Even better than the first time round."

"It's weird but somehow we always knew that the first album would be a Number One. Everything was going so fast then and our record was the sound of the time. It had to be Number One. And it was a real buzz, but nothing like this one. This feels special cos we've proved something to those people who'd written us off. We started at the top, went through some really low times and worked our way back up. We've proved ourselves."

"Everything just came together on this one," added Martin. "We could tell it was going to be this good right from when we started recording it. I don't know what it was exactly that made it different from what we've done before, it all just clicked. I don't think we could have done it better."

Looking back over The Charlatans' career, it was plain to see that, aside from their initial victory, which owed quite a lot to the whole scene which spawned them, they'd never fulfiled

Thirty Four

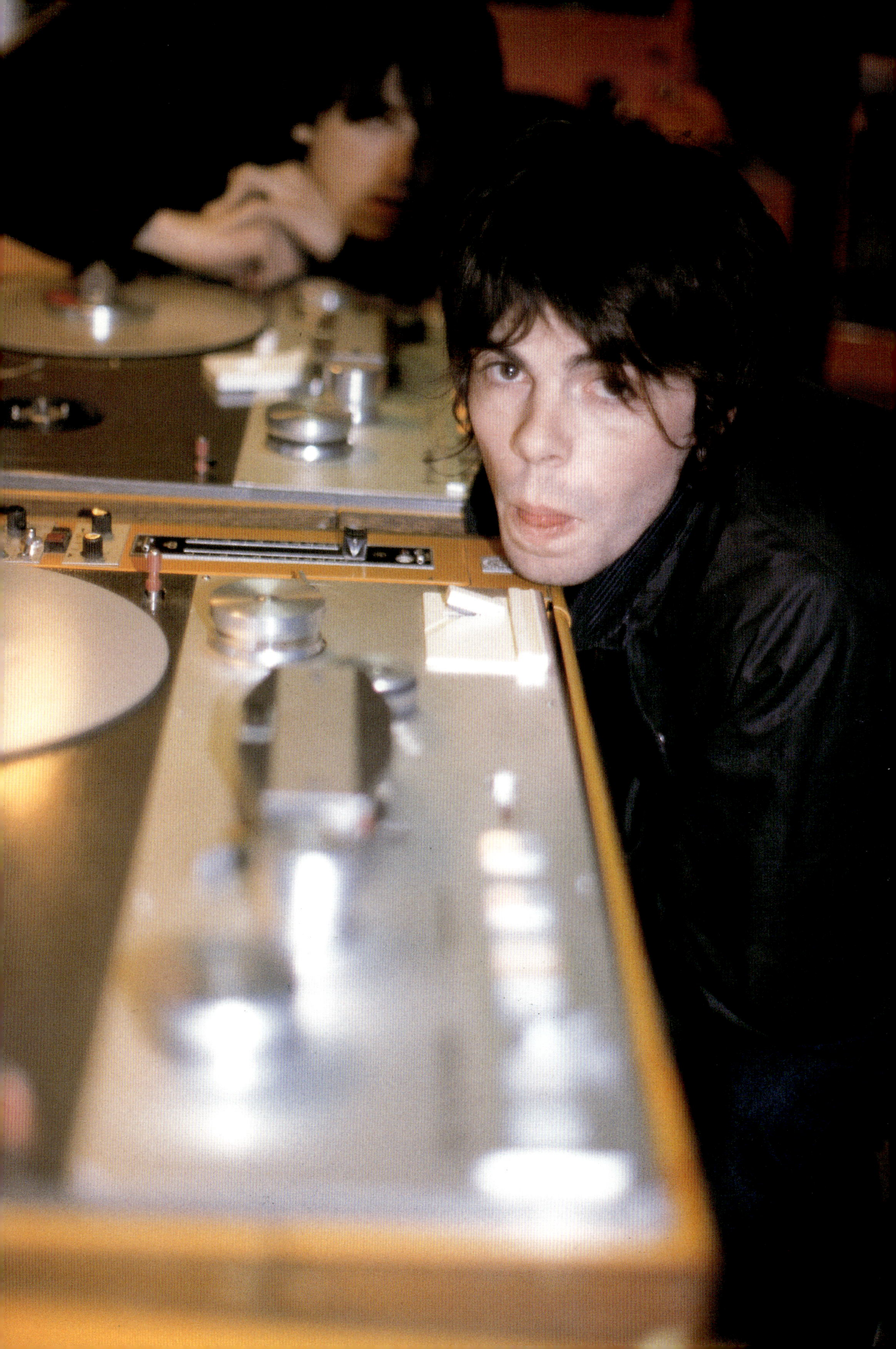

Thirty Six

their potential in the way in which they were now doing. And with hindsight, the band could clearly see where they'd slipped up, and where they'd been treated unfairly.

"We did have a problem being taken seriously because I think we let people take us for a ride a little bit," Jon told Sessions in 1997. "I think we made a lot of headlines, as all good groups should do. It was dead easy to go to jump on a train, go to Manchester, see The Charlatans and talk about everybody in the audience. Then, after people had got good print out of it, it became 'Oh yeah, it was all right at the time.' It's just funny how much people forget they were actually into it as well.

"When we first came out," continued Tim, "I thought we were going to do one LP and I just wanted to say loads of mad stuff. Now I wish I'd said things differently. But I was 22 and probably tried a bit hard. With a few knocks here and there, I think it's made us better. It made me better."

A Number One album on the back of a struggling career - which, no doubt, some thought was more or less over - was definitely proof that a few knocks had helped to consolidate the band as a unit, and clarify their musical direction.

"We're getting in people's faces," Tim told Music Week, "which has been one of our biggest criticisms, that we've never been that ambitious. I love the fact that The Charlatans release records and then go back into the studio and do some more and then go back out, release another one, tour it and go back and do some more. I love it - pretending to be Brian Wilson one night or Sly Stone the other night, George Best the night after."

"We've written proper songs," he enthused to Sun Zoom Spark. "There's a few that are a progression from 'Feel Flows' (from 'Up To Our Hips'). It's really raw and noisy and it's got loads of screaming on it."

Thirty Seven

"There's some really good songs on it too. It's got everything. Something for the boys and something for the girls. There's one called 'Bullet Comes' and it's the best song we've ever written."

Speaking of the hard time the band had been dealt by the British music press during their down phase, Tim sounded mature, considered and characteristically optimistic.

"It's made us get a grip of things. Everyone's taken it in turns and I think that's what makes us a proper band, what makes us in our heart of hearts better than the rest."

The main topic of conversation around the release of 'The Charlatans' was the question of survival - how the band had come through thick and thin, stuck together despite criticism, depressions and prison sentences, and eventually kicked right back with a number one album. Nobody had really expected it to happen, the press went into raptures and the band could barely believe their good fortune.

"We've always had a fight from day one," admitted Tim, **"The cynics saw us as chancers and yeah, for a while back there we were. I love the idea of stealing others' glories. But some people noticed that we meant everything we did. Deep down, they must have seen it in our eyes."**

Speaking with the Stud Brothers in a Melody Maker interview, Tim elaborated on the whole chancer idea.

"I always liked the idea that people thought we were charlatans because I always thought they meant we were like charming rogues who'd come along to take all the money. It always made me laugh. And it was good because it made us try harder. We always felt that, because of the Mondays and the Roses and the way we were seen in that whole Manchester thing, we had more to prove than anyone else."

Thirty Eight

THE CHARLATANS
NORTHWICH COUNTRY BOYS

Thirty Nine

STORY NUMBER TWO

So what exactly was The Charlatans' secret? How did they avoid disappearing in the mire? Having a strong and tightly knit line-up is one thing but there must have been more to keeping their heads above water.

"We avoided becoming a pastiche of ourselves," offered Martin to the NME's Johnny Cigarettes. **"And we knew the difference between cornering yourself into a genre and establishing your own sound, not based on fashion but an idea of real... soul music."**

"We've never, ever made music in our bedrooms," mused Jon. **"That's the difference I think, between us and so many cardboard, one-dimensional indie bands. It's organic, live music and it hits people in the heart and in the gut."**

"There is no one with an equity card in this band," continued Martin. **"None of us are backstage in our pipe and slippers preparing our 'act'. We are what we are on stage. And there's no students trying to be rebels. We always wanted to be a splash of colour to get away from black clothes, black attitudes and the Jesus And Fucking Mary Chain, and that's what we are."**

Speaking to i-D, Tim admitted that luck had played some part in the band's recovered success, but by no means the main part.

"We have surprised a lot of people. I think you can get lucky but you have to make it on your own. That's what we've learned, determination. That and never let an opportunity go to waste."

He also admitted that in their early stages, The Charlatans were hardly making life easy for themselves.

Forty

**THE CHARLATANS
NORTHWICH COUNTRY BOYS**

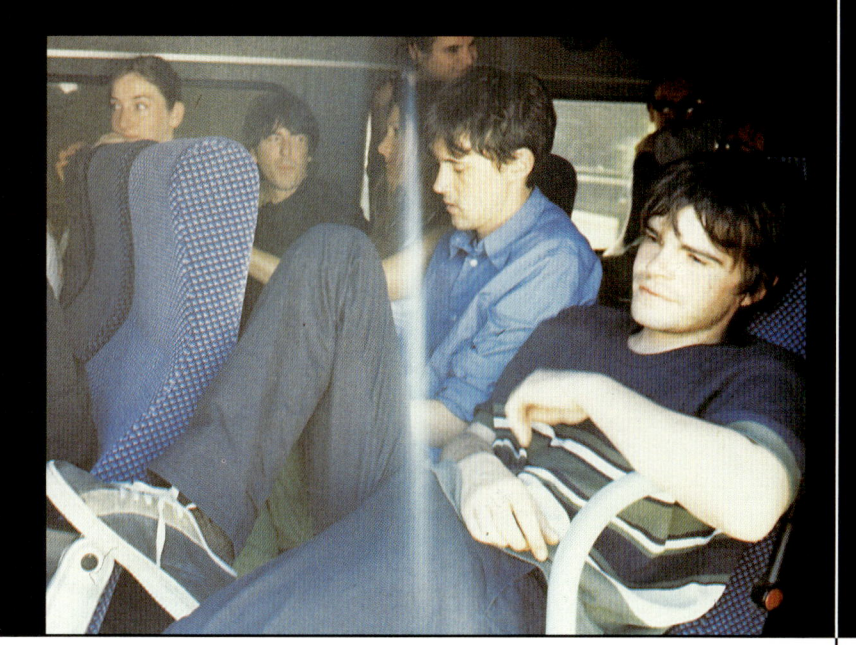

"Looking back, we didn't help ourselves. We didn't believe in shouting. We thought the music was good and that was enough. But we didn't think we needed anyone. We just felt it was gonna happen."

Mark's attitude was more philosophical, as Paul Mathur discovered.

"It never seemed like we'd run out of ideas or anything. I mean, there's some good songs on the last two albums, it's just that everyone else was out of step with what we were doing. We couldn't have made this record without going through what we did before and what happened to us."

The only real drawback to success is - what do you do if you lose it all again? How do you crawl back to a life of ordinariness when the dream falls apart? Not many rock stars seem to even consider this, unless they're just keeping schtum. But in 1995, Tim Burgess, eternal up-boy, was evidently thinking about the possibility of being forced back into his former reality. If someone considers the good - which, Tim had right from the start, entertaining one dream after another - they must also consider the bad, the bottom line being anything can happen.

"I worry about the consequences all the time," Tim confessed to i-D. "And my biggest fear is that the price is my girlfriend 'cos I love her. I've never felt as brilliant about anybody as I do about Chloe. She inspired the words and also she works for the press office, so she helped deliver it. I look at her as this Christ-like figure and I don't wanna lose that. But I'm sure there's a price to pay."

Speaking with the NME's Johnny Cigarettes, Tim continued his theme, but from a different perspective.

"What you've got to remember is that none of us have got anything to go back to. I mean, I'll never go back to where I was before, but I don't think the chance of me having to do something like that at one point has gone forever yet. I'm not dissing anyone who does, I just mean that I couldn't do it now."

Forty One

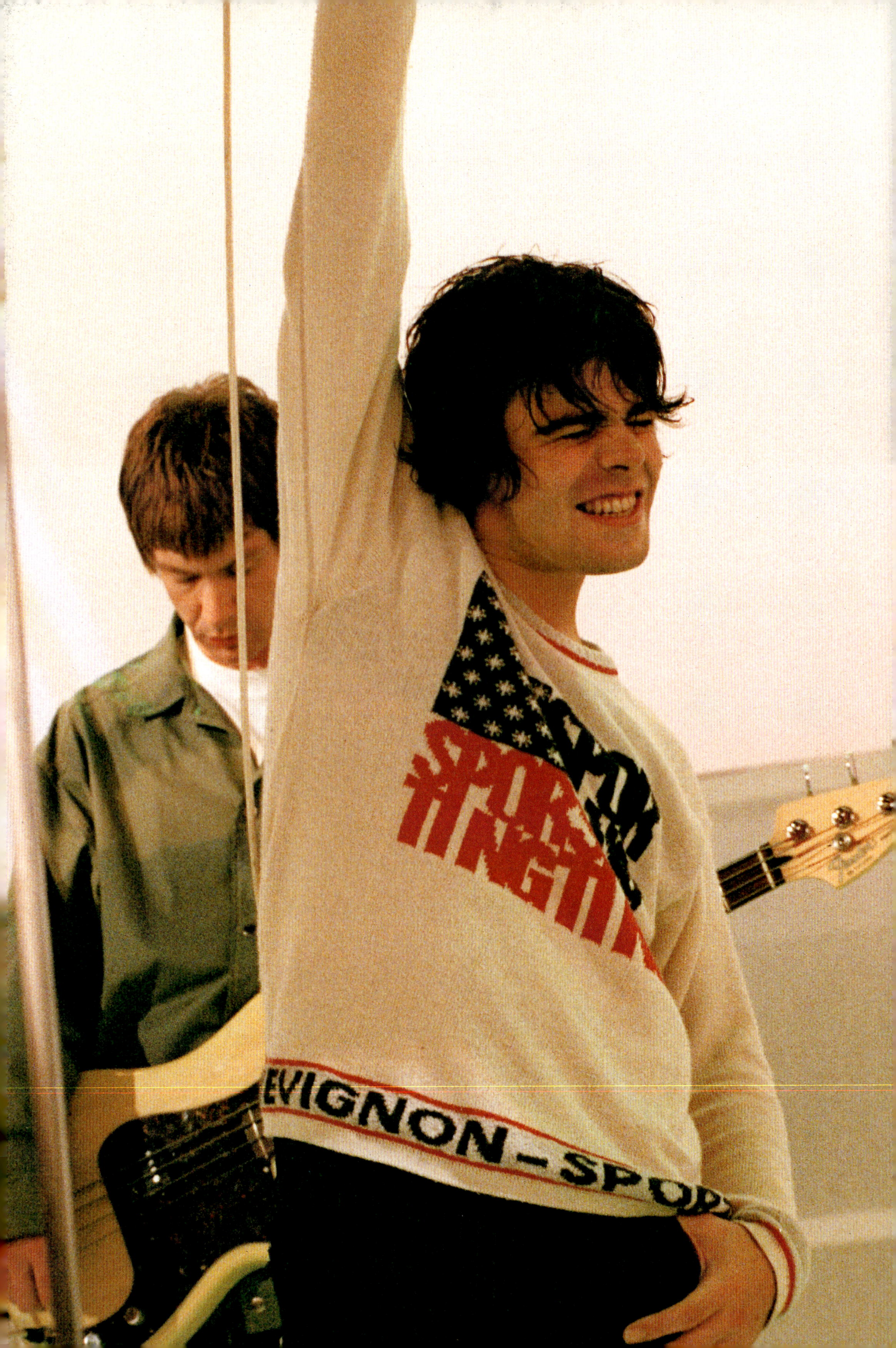
EVIGNON – SPOR

THE CHARLATANS
NORTHWICH COUNTRY BOYS

"It worries me because I spend money like there's no tomorrow. My biggest fear is having to go back and work in McDonald's. I think that's why I'm like I am. I'm always obsessed with not missing anything. Like even when we were recording the album, all the others would be in bed till about three and I'd be up really early just in case I might have been missing something. It's scary innit?"

"I get so disillusioned with people in bands when I find out that they're not as up for it as me, or that they don't want to go to the extremes. I mean, when I was a teenager working in ICI I'd look at the people in those bands whose records I bought and I wanted to trust them forever. When New Order said 'anyone can do it' in all those interviews, that was what motivated me in the first place. But I've always believed that there's got to be that degree of trust involved. I've never been into David Bowie for that reason. I can't get it, you know, it's too manipulative. But someone like Iggy, he went through everything, he tore his body apart."

"I can't imagine my life without being able to do what I love doing," he confessed to Paul Mathur. "It's what keeps me going, gets me up in the morning. This year, everything seems to have come together and I just go round thinking to myself 'this is brilliant!' This is all I've ever wanted to do and now I'm doing it. I tell you if I couldn't be doing this anymore, I'd be like one of those tramps out there crying in the street. I'd be gutted man."

"I don't like to think about doubts. I think what we've always done has come out of a kind of instinctive belief that it would work. And sometimes it hasn't, but we just forget it and go on to the next thing. I've got so many bits of songs going round in my head, loads of ideas, and I just have to get them out. I haven't got any choice. I really have to do this. I'd just die otherwise."

Forty Three

STORY NUMBER TWO

Tim's attitude was doubtless shared by each and every band member. All of them were involved in music for exactly the right reasons, and yes, this probably has had a lot to do with their survival. God knows the odds haven't exactly been on their side. When the band were due to tour America in 1995, cranberry juice makers, Ocean Spray, offered to sponsor them, but once they discovered Rob had been convicted of armed robbery, they withdrew their support.

"We went to meetings in New York City and we'd never gone into anything like that before," band manager Steve Harrison told the Melody Maker news desk in August of 1995. **"We were meant to be doing venues from about 1500, to 5,000 capacity, which is what we'd normally do, but going into a lot of the secondary markets where we might not otherwise play. Cranberry juice is a really big drink in America, and it gets easier to get into those secondary areas when you've got a well known name like Ocean Spray backing it up. But then we heard from our American record company that they'd just curtailed the idea like that, because of what Rob was involved in a couple of years ago."**

"We're not that concerned. We're now going to do our touring in the rest of the world and then back to America in December and do a full tour. But we spent weeks setting this up, and for someone to just make one phone call and pull it all from under us is a bit upsetting."

"I'm not condoning what Rob did for a moment, but there seem to be so many double standards over there. Their government is involved in so many wars and dubious activities, but one guy makes a mistake once in his life and that's it forever."

Trouble and America seemed to go together for The Charlatans. Just three months later, they flew from Canada to New York's JFK airport, and when they landed, they were arrested straight away by no less than 24 armed policemen and charged with "lewd and indecent

Forty Four

THE CHARLATANS
NORTHWICH COUNTRY BOYS

behaviour". Apparently, their party had been spitting and swearing at passengers, so six of them ended up in handcuffs actually on the plane. When the police found out about Rob's time in jail, the FBI were brought in.

"It was just fucking ridiculous," spat a disgusted Mark at the NME's Paul Moody. **"We were in economy class, scumbag class, right, and Tim had this bloke sitting in front of him who was obviously pissed off that his company hadn't paid for him to have a better seat. So when Tim started changing the channels on his TV, the guy thought Tim was deliberately annoying him, and he started putting his hands over the back of the seat and blocking the TV screen. We started messing around a bit, and next thing this guy shouted "Fuck off!" at Tim and threw a punch."**

"Then the crew joined in and it got a bit heated. The police arrived and handcuffed us all, then we went off to the cells and had to take off our shoelaces and belts in case we committed suicide. The funny thing was, Martin was asleep the whole time, and hadn't known anything about it until the police turned up on the plane."

"The only thing I saw was when it was all going off in mid-air and Rob Collins was strangling Johnny, our keyboard technician, because he'd forgotten to bring some valves for the organ," remembered Martin. **"I just saw him with his hands around his neck and Johnny's face going all purple."**

"It was nothing," said Mark. **"We have worse shit than that going down in the group every 24 hours. Fucking hell, it was a piece of piss, that."**

In the same interview, Tim echoed Mark's feelings on the incident. Put into perspective it was a very minor hitch. It was hardly going to affect the band's future.

Forty Five

**STORY
NUMBER TWO**

"People trust us, they know we're not going to let them down, no matter what. That's a really important thing about the group. We've been through a hell of a lot and people know about that and respect it. We've been through miles more than most bands anyway." Even the problems we've had on this tour, like getting arrested, are nothing compared to what we've been through generally. But don't ask me about what's happened to us recently 'cos I haven't got a fucking clue. But stuff that happened years ago, I'm all right with that."

Whatever problems The Charlatans had faced, they'd still found time to contribute to the War Child album, 'Help'. Conceived by Tony Crean of Go!Disc records, 'Help' saw all manner of artists coming together, including Paul Weller, Paul McCartney, Stone Roses, Radiohead, Sinead O'Connor, Terry Hall, Suede, Oasis and Johnny Depp, plus producers the Chemical Brothers and Brian Eno, to lay down tracks for charity. Within three days of going on sale, the album raised two million pounds, with all proceeds going towards providing help and care for the young victims of the war in Bosnia.

The Charlatans' track was a cover of Sly And The Family Stone's 'Time For Livin'', and with the Chemicals on production duty, it certainly stood out.

"This is the best track we've done," declared Tim, despite the fact that 'The Charlatans' had charted at number one just two days before. **"We've got to educate young people, young kids, that it's cool to care,"** he continued, speaking to Caspar Llewellyn Smith of The Daily Telegraph. **"We're not a political band but there's nothing wrong with this project. It's cool not to be selfish."**

'Help' was the fastest album to reach number one, notching up sales of 71,000 on its first day in the shops, and also the fastest recorded album, taking just six days to reach the top of the charts from commencement of work in the studio. Costs were kept right down, and record shops agreed to donate cuts as well as the artists. In the tradition of 'Live Aid', it has been the biggest pop charity event of its time, and The Charlatans were more than proud to be involved with it, as Tim had indicated.

"Music's there to be passed about," Tim told Melody Maker. **"And if it can put a dent in one hundred thousand people's heads with all the right information, so that people know what to do, then that's a real achievement."**

Forty Six

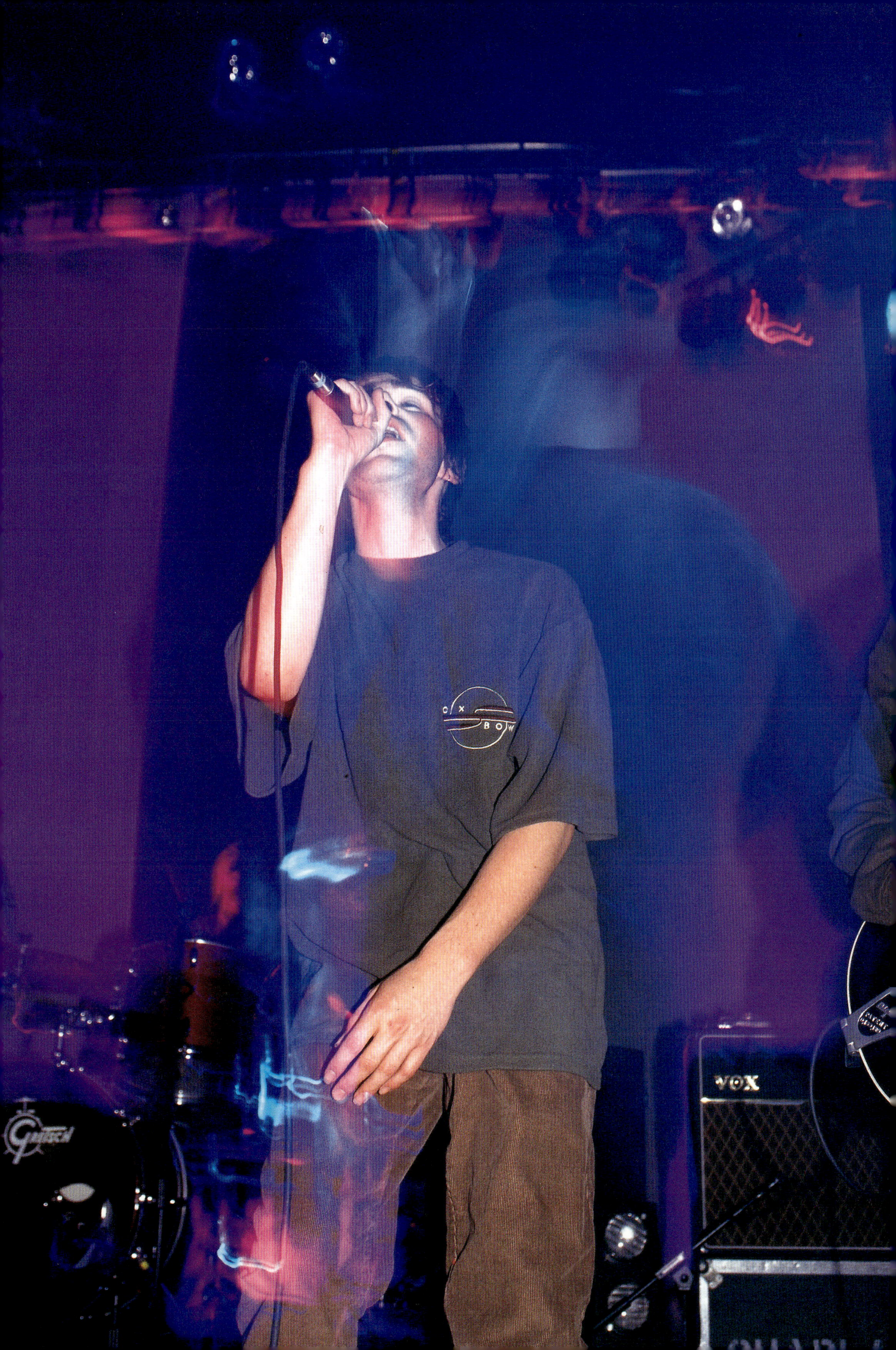
VOX

**STORY
NUMBER TWO**

THE CHARLATANS
NORTHWICH COUNTRY BOYS

QUIET
PLEASE

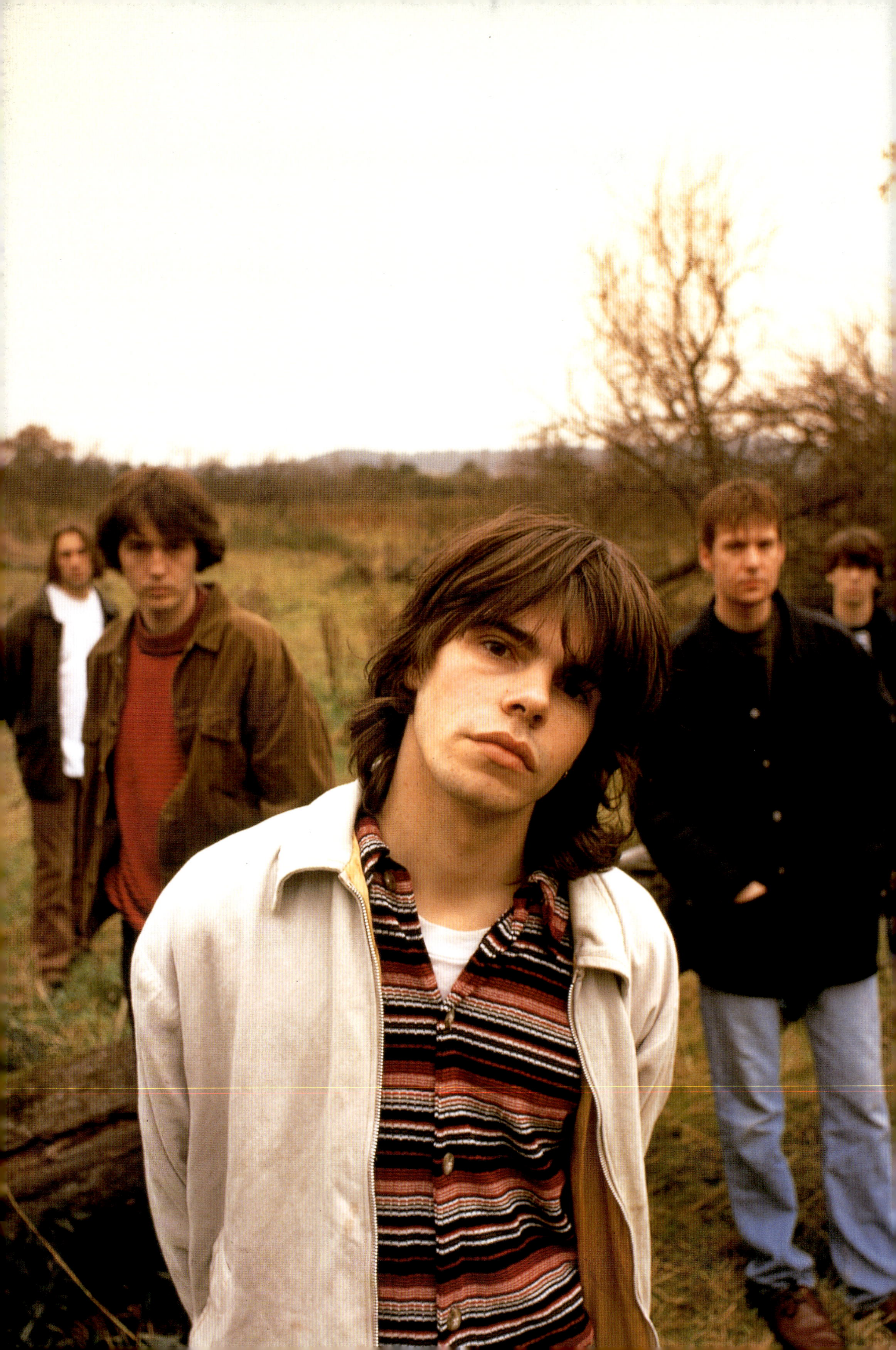

**THE CHARLATANS
NORTHWICH COUNTRY BOYS**

STORY NUMBER THREE

Nineteen ninety six was, without doubt, the most difficult year The Charlatans have ever faced. Its tragic events were to overshadow every trauma, every mishap, and every setback they'd been through so far, yet, in a strange, paradoxical fashion, they would also cement the band for once and all, and precede their biggest career success to date. 1996 was, for The Charlatans, going to be a year they would never ever forget.

Following the triumph of their fourth album, the band decided to record their fifth back at Monnow Valley Studios and the nearby Rockfield Studios, both in Monmouth, South Wales. They'd enjoyed it at Monnow Valley before, and the area was quiet and peaceful, away from possible distractions and interference. It seemed like the ideal spot from which to conjure up more of the brilliance which had rocketed through 'The Charlatans'.

By July, things were going well. The sessions sounded good and the band were on form. But at the end of the month, something happened which would alter the future irrevocably for all of them. On Monday 22nd, Rob Collins, keyboard player and enigmatic member of the band, was killed in a car crash.

Writing for Melody Maker, journalist Ben Stud, a close friend of the band, detailed the events leading up to Rob's death. His piece was the one which most accurately and movingly relayed the awful tragedy which befell The Charlatans that summer. Ringing with emotion, his article stood out from the more standard obituaries and remembrances, no doubt because it was written from a deeply personal, and therefore wounded, point of view.

Speaking with Ben, Jon Brookes recalled the last conversation he would ever have with his friend and band mate. It took place on the phone, on the Monday morning.

Fifty One

**STORY
NUMBER THREE**

THE CHARLATANS
NORTHWICH COUNTRY BOYS

"Every conversation I'd ever had with Rob would begin with a discussion about the music. Rob was utterly obsessed with the band. He wanted to know every tiny detail. That day, though, he sounded a little odd, like he was in a semi-coma or something. Which was sort of weird because he always had to be on top of things. So he rings me up and tells me he's still at home getting ready to go up to the studio. He wants to talk about some of the ideas he's got for some of the songs. So we chat about that for a while, and I'm saying that some of the keyboard stuff he's put down recently sounds a little bit wishy-washy. And he gets a little bit uppity about that."

"He didn't take too well to criticism, did Rob. Then he starts kind of agreeing with me and the conversation ends with me telling him to get stuck in. I told him I'd be there in a while. And that was about it. I wished him luck and that. But there was something odd. He sounded so slow and quiet, like it was one heartbeat an hour. That was the last time I ever spoke to him."

Tim Burgess recalled how Rob had arrived at Monnow Valley that Monday evening, at around 6pm.

"He was miserable as ever. No more or less so than at any other time. He was just Rob, you know, slagging everything off, taking the piss. He was ready for work as far as I was concerned. Thing is, it was this mate of ours' birthday, so we decided to go and celebrate. It's like this guy had waited all day for Rob to turn up so we could all have a drink together.

"By about nine, it was fucking manic in the pub, man. You know what I'm saying? We were all just mad for it. Everyone was having a great time. Even Rob was more fucking social than usual. He was happy as fuck 'cos he's just won sixty quid on the fruit machine. I mean, he was off his fucking head, having a top night out, and he wins all this fucking money."

Fifty Three

**STORY
NUMBER THREE**

"See, when Rob went down the pub, he wasn't exactly social. He was quiet. His thing was stuffing money into machines. He'd stand there, with his pint on top of the machine, staring at the fruit. But that night, he was jumping about all over the place. He were dead fucking happy. So anyway around ten o'clock, I've got to get back and put some vocals down. Rob tells me to take his car back to the studio and order him a cab to come and pick him up. I got into his car and ... Ah, fuck it! The fucking hand brake went off didn't it? I ended up bumping this fucking car in front. So I thought, I'm not fucking driving this man, I mean, I haven't driven for five fucking years and after that fucking hand brake going off, I just didn't trust myself behind the wheel."

"So I took the keys back and said 'I can't fucking drive this, man.' I get into someone else's car, get back to the studio and get on with me singing and that."

After another hour in the pub, Mark Collins, Rob and everyone else headed back to the studio after Tim. Mark thought about driving back with Rob, but decided against it, ironically enough because he didn't think it would be exciting enough. Instead, he wanted to ride in his friend's car because he thought it would be more fun.

"A friend of ours had this old Granada. It was a really cool one, like you see in old telly programmes like 'The Sweeney'. We'd been watching that GTI advert where you got the two blokes taking the piss out of 'The Professionals', so we just spent the weekend racing round these little lanes doing hand brake turns and stuff."

The Granada left ahead of Rob, whose car had been crammed in by two others parking too close to him. He bashed them out of the way, triggering off their alarms, and set off, angry and frustrated. Almost immediately he caught up with the others, who thought he was playing one of his games on them. Apparently he'd do things like that, he used "to drive at things, or fucking creep up on you" according to Jon. So perhaps Rob was trying a race-chase game.

Fifty Four

No one knows. All that they remember is that just as suddenly as they'd appeared, his headlights vanished. Everyone assumed he'd taken a short cut, as part of the game he was probably playing. Or that he'd stopped for cigarettes.

It was in Rob's nature to play games. Drinking games, racing games, mind games. And dead games. Either he would disappear for days on end, without explanation, or he'd play dead in the bath, in bed, with his girlfriend Rachel, or around the band. He enjoyed the wind-up.

"He used to do it all the time," Tim told Ben. **"You'd bring him a cup of tea in the morning, or something, and he'd be lying there totally still. You'd shake him and he'd be totally limp. And you'd be like, 'fuck off, Rob. Behave.' And the bastard would suddenly come to and start laughing his bollocks off."**

Rob was certainly a character. On the road with the band in Canada, NME journalist Paul Moody discovered how Rob had thrown all of his tour laminates out of the window of the van on the way to Heathrow airport, how he'd ripped up all of his tour itineraries on arrival in the States, and how in Montreal, he'd ripped his hotel door off its hinges.

On another occasion, Rob had been sharing a hotel room with Martin Blunt, when, in the middle of the night, the fire alarm went off. Rather than get dressed and leave the building, Rob simply tore the alarm from the wall, threw it in the wardrobe, and went back to sleep.

"He just didn't give a shit," said Martin.

When Rob's headlights disappeared from the road behind Mark and Tim's mate's Granada, it had nothing to do with one of the keyboard player's games. This wasn't a wind-up. Rob had lost control of his BMW, hit a kerb, slid across the road, smashed through a hedge and hurled over a bank. He wasn't wearing a seat belt, and was thrown through the windscreen. Later, Jon found out that Rob had managed to get up on his feet, bleeding profusely from his neck and face, before collapsing. According to Ben, this was the image which would endure for The

Fifty Five

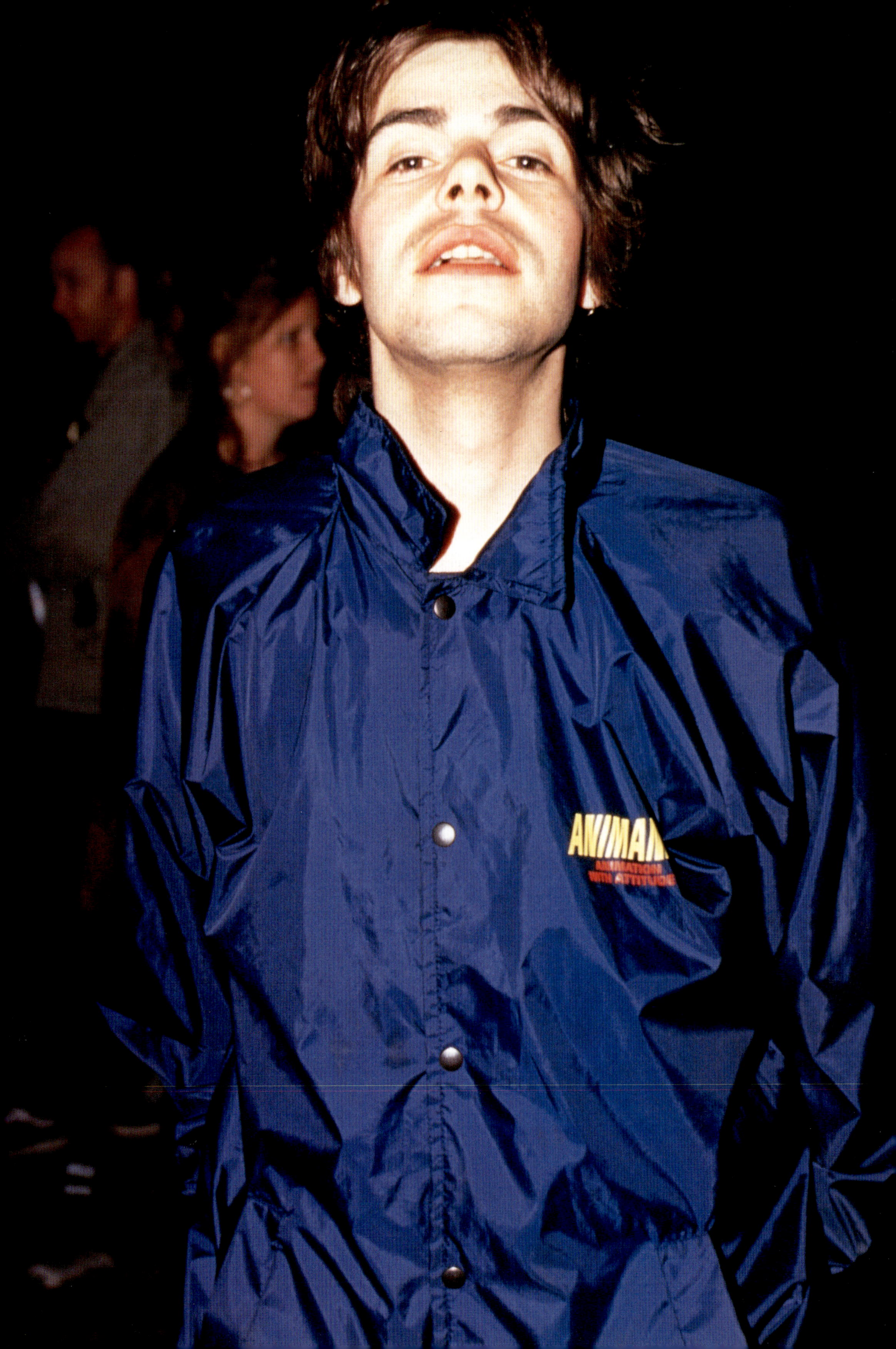
ANIMAN

THE CHARLATANS
NORTHWICH COUNTRY BOYS

Charlatans, this image of Rob fighting to stay alive. In the end, it was a factor in their decision to keep going as a band.

A woman who lived in a neighbouring cottage had heard the crash and telephoned the police. She rushed out to try and revive Rob, but he died in the ambulance on the way to Abergavenny Hospital.

When the police turned up on Rob's girlfriend, Rachel's doorstep, on Tuesday morning at 1am, to tell her the news, she refused to believe them. She was convinced it was another of his games, and at first simply laughed at them.

"It's just a pisstake," she said. **"Don't believe him. He's fine. He's always doing things like this."**

Eventually she realised that this wasn't a pisstake. This time it was for real.

On the night of Rob's death, Jon had gone to bed early, but couldn't get to sleep.

"I was lying there with my girlfriend," he told Ben, **"and it was really hot. I was just laying there looking at my clock and getting more and more restless. At about 11.30 I think 'fuck this.' So I pick up my book, go downstairs, put the TV on, put the kettle on and plonk myself down next to the phone."**

"At around midnight I turn the TV off and the phone goes. Now I think it's Rob, 'cos he always used to ring me at daft hours of the day and night to talk gibberish. Especially when he'd had a drink. Anyway I pick up the phone and it's Steve Harrison, our manager. So I'm like, 'All right, man. What's up?' He tells me there's been an accident. Immediately I say, 'Yeah, Rob.' Steve says 'I've spoken to the police. The guy in the car with Rob is fine, but Rob's in a bit of a state.' Steve said he'd call me back when he'd had some more information."

Fifty Seven

STORY NUMBER THREE

"I'm not a religious person, but I felt... compelled to pray. I did, man. I swear to God I just fucking knew something fucking terrible had happened. I mean, I've seen Rob do a lot of crazy fucking stuff. I've seen him have fights. I've seen him in a lot of scrapes. I've seen him in violent arguments. I've seen him kick stuff about and smash things up and chuck shit out of windows. I've seen him doing all sorts of mad stuff, but never once did I ever think he would wind up dead. This time it was different. I just sat there on the couch with the phone in my hand and heard myself praying for his soul."

"I envisioned him lying on one of those stretcher things, a bit cut up, a bit fucked up and I thought, 'Rob, if you're still there, hang in, fight it, you'll be OK. The doctors will sort you out. Just fight it.' Twenty minutes later, I'm pacing about the fucking house and the phone goes again. Steve tells me he's dead."

Jon put the phone down, poured himself a big glass of wine, and went upstairs to wake his girlfriend.

"She was really sleepy. I don't think she heard me the first time I said it. I had to repeat it a couple of times. She wakes up and she's the same as me, sort of dazed. I asked her to run me to the garage to get some cigarettes. By this time it was getting light. When I got home it hit me. He was dead. It hit me like a ton of fucking bricks. I started putting records on."

Back in Wales, Tim and Mark were faced with the situation.

"Mark gets back to the studio and Rob ain't there," Tim told Ben. "So now we're all positive he's stopped off on the way back. He might've popped into Rockfield 'cos he had a lot of mates there, or he might have gone on some mad fucking country drive, which he used to do occasionally. At any rate, we just assumed he was gonna turn up later and get on with the stuff he'd come up to do.

Fifty Eight

"What happens then is that we get a phone call saying that Rob's been in a car crash. It was a mate of ours that called. I think he'd actually gone looking for him. He calls up around midnight. He'd seen the car wreck and the ambulances and he clocked what had happened. So he rushed into Rockfield to ring me and Mark. All we knew then was that he'd been taken to hospital. Shortly after that, we got a visit from the police."

"The first thing I remember them saying to me was 'How old is he?' and I hear 'How bald is he?' I'm thinking what the fuck is going on? What the fuck are they on about? You know I'm pissed and a little dazed, and I just don't know what the fuck is going on. But I'm still not thinking the worst. The police are just asking a load of questions. Mark's doing his usual bit, walking round casual as fuck, trying to bully the police and take the piss out of them and that. I'm just fucking dazed."

"But I did kind of get an inkling. I remember them saying 'What instrument did he play?' And I thought they're using the past tense. So I go 'He fucking plays keyboards.' But it was only fleeting. It came at me, but I didn't really realise what they meant. I did, but I didn't. I don't remember dwelling on it."

"The two coppers tell me and Mark that Rob's been a bit of a naughty boy. Those were their words, 'naughty boy'. They tell us that we should go and visit him. It took us about an hour to get to hospital. We were driving like mad-heads. I'm sitting in the car singing 'One To Another' to myself. Just singing it in my head. You know, like trying to stop myself from thinking too much. But I've got this nagging little fucking voice that keeps jumping in and saying 'He's fucking dead, he's fucking dead.' And I'm saying to myself, 'Bollocks is he.'"

"By the time we get to hospital, I've virtually convinced myself he's fine."

Fifty Nine

STORY NUMBER THREE

Mark went through the hospital doors ahead of Tim, also convinced that Rob must be all right. But when a nurse showed him into a room, it became apparent that maybe he wasn't after all. The nurse broke the news to Mark, and he, in turn, had to tell Tim. The only way he could believe it was to repeat it over and over to himself, like a mantra as Ben put it. And finally it sank in.

Initially the band had absolutely no idea what to do. They'd lost one of their best friends, not just a band member, and they were utterly shattered.

"We were all over the place," Tim recalled later. **"We couldn't string sentences together half the time. We were probably close to calling it a day."**

A phone call from Rob's dad soon put paid to any ideas of quitting though. Because, after all, it wouldn't have been what Rob would have wanted.

"There's no point in giving it all up," Martin told Ben Stud on the telephone, the Friday following the accident. **"Things are never going to be the same again, but we do want to carry on. We know it's the right thing to do."**

Rob's father had telephoned Steve Harrison to tell him that his son would have wanted The Charlatans to continue. Everyone met up at Harrison's house on the Friday afternoon to kickstart themselves back into action. Their date at Loch Lomond, supporting Oasis had already been cancelled, but they decided to go ahead with the Knebworth show and drafted in Primal Scream's Martin Duffy to help out on keyboards. They also put together a statement which was issued to the press. Its closing words were; "There will be no change. We are fucking rock. We've lost our mate."

The Knebworth show was hard, the Chelmsford V96 festival was hard. Tim kept looking round expecting to see Rob, but he kept seeing Martin instead. Old friends were in tears, just as they had been at Rob's cremation just outside Wolverhampton. But ultimately the band knew they had made the right decision to carry on. They didn't dedicate any of their songs to Rob, because as Martin later put it, from now on everything they did would be dedicated to him, and besides, they didn't want to be seen to be cashing in on his death in any way. The respect they felt was far too great.

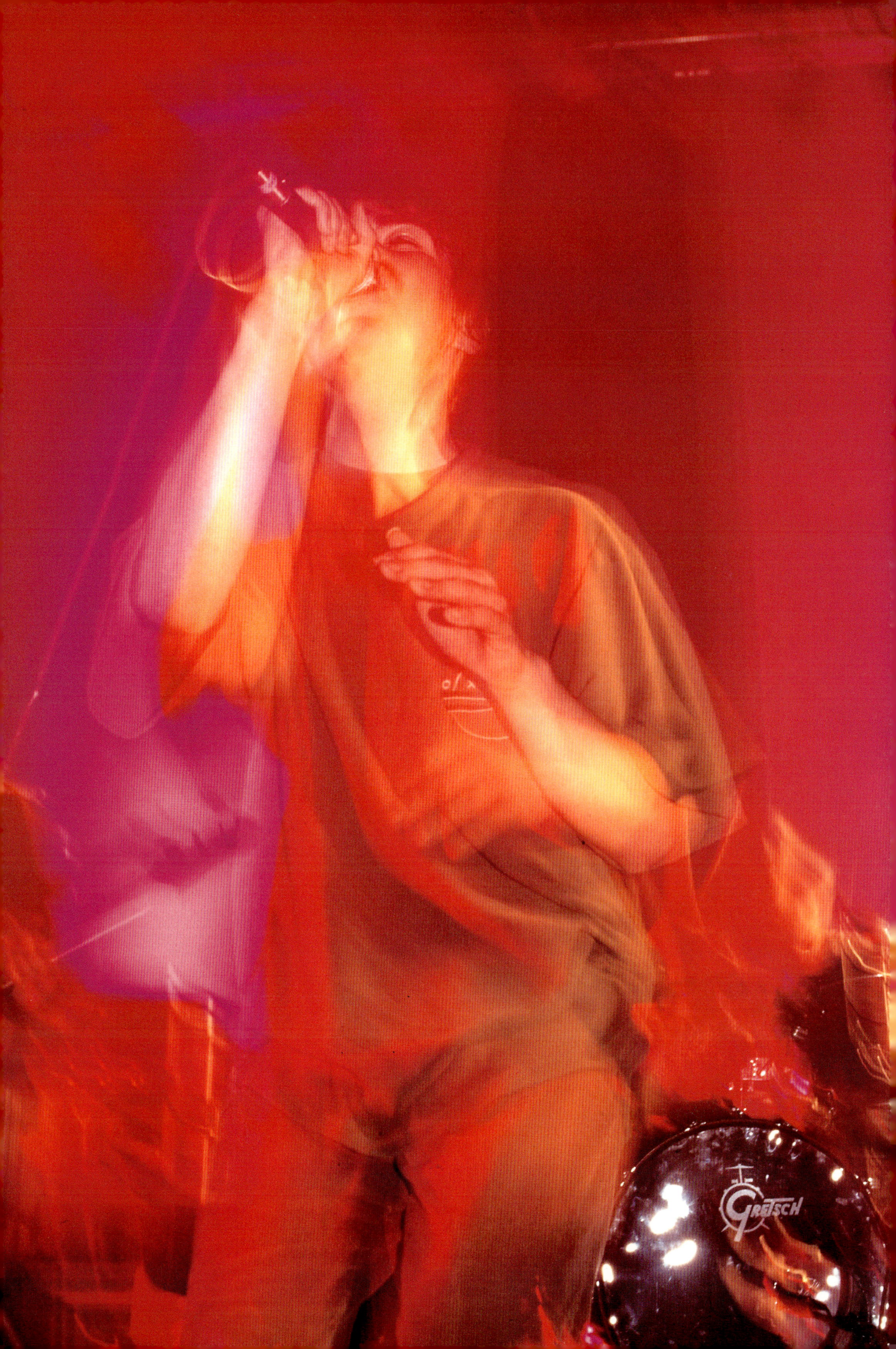
GRETSCH

**STORY
NUMBER THREE**

THE CHARLATANS
NORTHWICH COUNTRY BOYS

Seven months after Rob's death, The Charlatans completed their fifth album, 'Tellin' Stories'. They'd finished it with the help of Martin Duffy, and were feeling confident about it, even though they were still coming to terms with their loss.

"There was a bit of a weird week," Tim told Andrew Mueller for The Independent.

"For a few days after Rob died we didn't really know what was going on and we just went through every possible emotion you could, but I think we always wanted to finish the album. We knew there was really good stuff in there, and even if we hadn't ever finished it, I think the record company would have put it out anyway. So it made sense to get the best out of it and we did. And now we can start afresh. It's got to be different now because there's only four of us. We'll all have to stretch our imagination a bit more."

It was around this time - early 1997 - that Tony Rodgers stepped in to fill the keyboard spot. Initially he was drafted in temporarily, largely because The Charlatans needed time to adjust. Martin Duffy was committed to Primal Scream, and they definitely needed someone for their forthcoming tour of Britain, and as he was one of just two 'Hammond whizzkids' that they discovered, they held onto him.

This was a very peculiar time for the band. 'Tellin' Stories' was a celebrated album, 'a thing of incredulous life-affirming joy' as Mueller described it, and yet here it was, released just a few months after the death of one of their best friends. Despite everything though, The Charlatans, still found time to feel positive.

"Ever since the start of The Charlatans I never thought we'd do more than one or two albums, but after that it was like... yeah!" Tim said to Luke Bainbridge for City Life magazine. **"And since then we've only looked one ahead and I think that's the best way really.**

Sixty Three

STORY NUMBER THREE

"I've been through a lot mate, y'know what I mean? I got fucking chucked by my girlfriend at the start of the album sessions, and then one of my best friends dies, but through all that we still managed to have a bit of fun... it's just what came through. I knew what I wanted to do more than I did on the last LP, then I thought I'd lost it halfway through, but I realised at the end that it was good.

"You know when you were a kid and you were growing up and you thought that you'd be cast in stone forever? That's what I want, man. I think that's what we've always wanted. It's just taken us ages to realise our own potential."

Speaking to Ted Kessler for Vox, Tim reiterated his point. **"We all know that we've got a better place to get to musically, and Rob's part of that too, because we'd recorded 12 songs with him when he died. I know what we've lost is big, but I know that what we'll get is big. So it's phase two..."**

Lyrically, as well as musically, 'Tellin' Stories' was probably the best delivery to date. Tim's words had often appeared to be about not very much at all, but with this new album, they were very obviously about emotions, relationships, and of course Rob.

"I'm finding a lot of solace in Tim's lyrics right now," admitted Jon in the Vox interview.

So what was Tim singing about?

"Everything real. Give it to 'em real. And raw. Just about people and me and the world. Every song tells a story," Jon continued. **"And we've tailored the music around the lyrics and I think that works really well."**

Tim saw his new lyrics as conversations. He adopted a mental image of a squirrel, chilling out, smoking weed, and observing everything beneath him, in much the same way as De La Soul used the image of a wise old crocodile on their 'Tread Water' track. His split with long-time and

Sixty Four

THE CHARLATANS
NORTHWICH COUNTRY BOYS

Sixty Five

STORY
NUMBER THREE

THE CHARLATANS
NORTHWICH COUNTRY BOYS

much beloved girlfriend, Chloe, also seemed to have been an important influence, although he didn't exactly say as much. But 'One To Another' is about a boy trying to stop his relationship from collapsing, and 'North Country Boy' is sees the guy trying to cheer himself up.

"The guy in the song - it's me innit," Tim confessed to NME journalist, Stuart Baillie. **"After losing a lot and offering so much, the song has become a love and forgiveness tune really. The mood is up and down, just like the singing really."**

"I was thinking about the Bob Dylan song, 'Girl From The North Country' but I centred it around a bloke. We have people coming in and saying 'it's a Manchester song' but it's not. Fuck knows where the north country was when Bob Dylan was singing about it."

'Tellin' Stories' was to be The Charlatans' last album for their record label, Beggars Banquet. Having decided they could do with a change, the band opted to continue their career with MCA after A&R man, John Walsh, fended off some severe competition to win them.

"We wanted to change labels because we felt that it was time for us to move on," explained Mark to Music Week's Lisa Verrico. **"We need new impetus and we think the band would benefit from the bigger push of a major label. We went with MCA because they were the most on our wavelength. They didn't want to disrupt anything or put us in with big name producers. We asked for complete control and they were happy to give us that."**

Naturally Beggars were sorry to see them go, but they were also pleased that they'd had the chance to enjoy such a good relationship with the band, and also, that with 'Tellin' Stories', things were ending on a high.

During the springtime of 1997, The Charlatans went out on tour around Britain to promote their new album. The shows were a resounding success, culminating in a truly uplifting all-nighter at

Sixty Seven

**STORY
NUMBER THREE**

London's Brixton Academy in aid of the National Missing Person's Helpline. Also on the Brixton bill were Smaller, James Dean Bradfield of the Manic Street Preachers, surprise guest Paul Weller, even more of a surprise guest Noel Gallagher, and DJs from the Big Kahuna Burger and Heavenly Jukebox nightclubs. The night couldn't have been better, and served as further proof not only of The Charlatans' concern for worthy causes (after all, the whole subject of loss and helplessness was particularly close to their hearts) but also that they had just handed the world their best collection of songs yet - as the translation in the live arena testified.

"The thing is," said Martin, **"this record really is the business. It feels so right and sounds good. It's like a cross between Dexys' 'Searching For The Young Soul Rebels' and 'Let It Bleed' by the Stones. That's the spirit behind it. And our belief is as strong as it was seven years ago. It's spiritual. And I don't think cynicism has eaten away at the group the way it could've done."**

"What's the point in being cynical anyway?" Mark rightly pointed out. **"Enjoy life. You only get the one."**

Sixty Eight

CHAPTER ONE
NORTHWICH COUNTRY BOYS

THE CHARLATANS
NORTHWICH COUNTRY BOYS

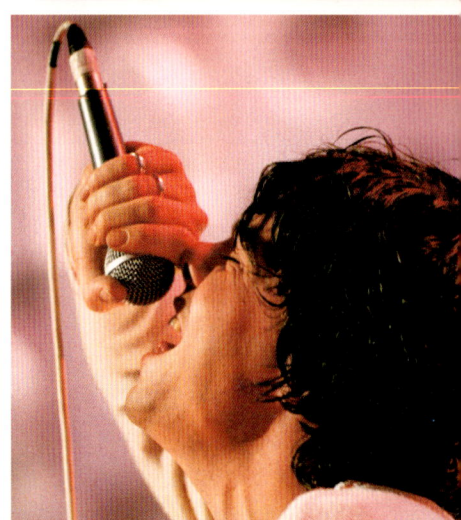